Lady of Isan

The Story of a Mixed Marriage
from Northeast Thailand

MICHAEL SCHEMMANN

ThaiSunset Publications

www.ThaiSunset.com

LADY OF ISAN
The Story of a Mixed Marriage from Northeast Thailand

Second edition and reprint 2007

The National Library of Thailand
Cataloguing-in-Publication Data

Schemmann, Michael
  Lady of Isan. Story of a Mixed Marriage from Northeast
  Thailand
  Pattaya: ThaiSunset Publications
  151 pp.
   16 color plates
  1. Isan – Mixed Marriage

  ISBN 974-93678-7-1

Published by
ThaiSunset Publications
www.ThaiSunset.com
Email thaisunset@gmail.com

Dedicated to my wife Iuu with Love and Devotion.

Bangkok, June 2004

Sorrow is better than laughter; for by the sadness of the face the heart is made good.

Ecclesiastes 7:3

CONTENTS

Prologue 6

1 Moving to Thailand 7

2 Pattaya Seminar 10

3 Udon Thani 17

4 Our Wedding Day 24

5 First Year at ABAC 29

6 Second Year at ABAC 44

7 Caring for Mother 49

8 Third Year at ABAC 62

9 Literature Review 75

10 The Rough Year 2004 79

11 Enduring Her Father 89

12 Troubled Waters 99

13 Hide and Seek 107

14 The Finale 118

15 At Last 130

16 Epilogue 136

Foreword to the corrected "Second Edition" and Reprint

The purpose of the first edition of this story was therapeutic. It was written in a couple of weeks of extreme agony in Bangkok during April and May of 2004 after my young Lady of Isan had, yes - run away. I needed a medium to talk to her because in her typical barbaric fashion she had slapped a brutal no-contact ban on me.

The second purpose was to win her back. The booklet has "magnificently" succeeded… followed by the sequel entitled *Lady of Pattaya*.

Lady of Isan is a beach book. It sold the entire first printing in one season. This reprint is by popular demand, and also to make minor corrections.

The booklet enjoyed several reviews, one thanks to Lang Reid of the Bangkok Post and the Pattaya Mail saying:

The book is a diary of the intense personal feelings of a middle aged farang, who falls for this 19 year old Isan girl.

[The book] will not grace the lists of literary masterpieces of the decade... [but] is not an expensive salutary lesson, and certainly very much cheaper than author Schemmann's lesson in Thai life...

I know from experience that readers are motivated more by a harsh critique than one that is blandly favorable.

Nakhon Ratschasima, June 2007

Prologue

After the limo had taken you home in the early hours of Sunday morning, May 27, 2001, I returned to the hotel room feeling numb and empty inside. Then I found your silver necklace. It was lying on the bathroom counter under a couple of white towels. I held it in my palm wondering for a while who might have given it to you as a token of promises to come, or his gratitude for your love.

Then I began studying your name and address that you had written in beautiful clean Thai letters on the hotel stationary just minutes before you left, and I was lost. The only words I could decipher without fail were "Iuu" written in Thai, LOVES "Michael", also written in Thai.

Did I want anyone else's help to translate your writing for me? No.

"I will learn your language," I said to myself. "I will learn your vowels and consonants on the wings of love and with the speed and ease that my mother had taught me hers when I was just a child."

"You and I and our child", I was sure that's what you meant when you put your finger first on my mouth and then your belly, saying with wishful determination:

"Baby", pronouncing it "baybeeh".

The postal code on your Thai address was the only hint of your village near Udon Thani on the desolate high plateau in Northeast Thailand, which the Thais call Isan.

At the end of my teaching term in Bangkok, in early September, I intended to look you up and meet your family: your penniless 42-year old mother and your father for whom you work the nights away in Pattaya in the arms of *farangs* like me.*Phom rak khun.* You are so easy to love.

Chapter 1
Moving to Thailand

Assumption University of Thailand in Bangkok was the first to reply to my emails to the universities of Thailand, offering me a teaching position as visiting professor in the Graduate School of Business for a term of four months at a dismal $4,000 payable at the end of the term for two courses: Managerial Accounting, and International Financial Management.

The time was mid-March 2001. Their question was whether I wanted to start in May or in August. It was raining outside my rented room in Vancouver, British Columbia, on Canada's West Coast, the temperature around 10 degrees, still snow on the mountains. I replied without hesitation: "May".

On the last day of April, my son, Armin, drove me to the airport at around midnight. It was a clear and crisp moonlit night. Looking back at the city to the east and the mountains in the background was an impressive sight. Jets screaming overhead coming in for landings and taking off, coming and going to places in Canada, the United States and the world, gave me a good feeling about myself. I was on the move again after thirteen years in this city, nine of which I had spent alone following my separation from wife number two and our two young boys.

"I may return a married man," I said to Armin. He answered "ahum", not knowing what to think of my remark.

I had been to Thailand on a ten-day stop over from Tokyo to Frankfurt twenty-three years earlier when I was still married to wife number one. I remembered how deeply satisfied and happy I had been in Chiang Mai spending a few days with a 22-year old almond tanned lotus girl, a beautiful and tender working lady, and how she had transformed my backed-up sex life into complete relaxation and joy. I kept the memory well lodged in the back of my mind for many years, always intent on returning one day. She would be forty-five now and well over the hill, I thought to myself.

The night flight across the immense Pacific to Hong Kong was uneventful. On the last leg to Bangkok I sat next to a middle-aged English couple, both working for Cathay Pacific Airlines, on their way to visit their son who was working in the south of Thailand and enjoying himself. They told me a bit about the traffic jams in Bangkok, the pollution, the abject poverty in the suburbs, and lots of other negative things that I already knew and didn't want to hear at this stage.

I like landing in the tropics. The sun's intense radiation turns the colors of the lush vegetation, city and landscape into an immensely aluminous and happy picture, especially for someone used to the discrete pastel tones of the northern climes. Arriving in the tropics, including Hawaii, always gave me a great boost of energy not felt in the north, until the heat and humidity upon leaving the airplane hit me in the face and covered my entire body with an instant sweat. Most northerners, after living in Thailand for many years, still admit that they cannot get used to the heat. But air conditioning is everywhere, in the cars, the offices, and city homes, but not in the villages.

The university's limo picked me up at the airport and whisked me in an hour over elevated freeways to the old city campus in Hua Mak, District of Bangkapi in Bangkok. I was led to my studio room on the twelfth floor of Queen's Tower that had a gorgeous view of the entire skyline of Bangkok to the west. I had a balcony, a bathroom, a nook in the wall with a desk to serve as my office, and a decent queen-size bed. I took a long shower and then collapsed on the bed.

After three days of catching up on my jet lag, wandering through the campus noticing the abundance of pretty young Thai ladies dressed in white shirts and black skirts with slightly slit dark eyes, almond skin and long black hair, and taking buses through the city to get a feel for my new place, classes began. I had a group of about twenty-five students in the accounting class, and fifteen in the finance class. Three hours each on two separate days of the week and I was done. The staff was very polite and I made a few instant friends among the visiting American, Australian and English faculty.

An American colleague, a somewhat opinionated loud-mouth by the name of Jeff, had been to Bangkok before and volunteered to show me the nightlife because he felt horny, he said. We took a taxi to the new sex business district of Nana on Sukhumvit Road, visited a couple of beer bars and bars with nude dancers hopping around steel poles ("go-go bars"). They were young Thai girls with long hair, small to medium size breasts and seemed quite erotic. Jeff explained to me that I could take anyone to an hour-hotel for a bar fine of 400 baht ($10) plus whatever I was willing to pay them, may be another 500 up to 1,000 baht, but no more he said, otherwise I would spoil the prices for the rest of us. After two or three hours of hanging around, commenting on this one and that one, we went home.

I met the Dean, Brother Vinai, dressed in a white Catholic monk's robe, an alert and inquisitive man in his forties with a good sense of humor. He welcomed me to his graduate school of business and said the faculty would go to Pattaya on a weekend seminar with the intake of MBA students at the end of the month, and that would be a lot of fun. As it turned out it was, and then some. That weekend would change my life, relieve me of old emotional baggage of the past that I had carried for the past nine years, and give Thailand a new perspective for my future.

Chapter 2
Pattaya Seminar

ABAC's minibus left campus at seven o'clock in the morning. The two-hour drive along the motorway to Pattaya was delightful. I sat next to Miss Dr. Chittipa, a lecturer in her early forties, still single and quite keen on having a lively conversation with me. She was of Chinese origin, she said, and had been a student at ABAC herself at one time.

The seminar was at the Royal Cliff Beach Resort, Thailand's finest. I got a large single room with a double bed on the 9th floor above the swimming pool overlooking the bay, stretched out for half an hour and then joined the crowd for the opening address by our president, Reverend Brother P. Martin Komolmas, a steely but benign 72-year old monk of the Brothers of Saint Gabriel who had built up ABAC from it's dismal state in the early 70's to its present renown and glory.

There was a guest speaker, the former minister of finance of the Royal Thai government who had cut the baht loose from its misconceived 25 baht per US dollar peg in July 1997 at the height of the Asian financial crisis and been sacked as a result. Now the baht was floating at a cut below 45 baht to the dollar holding firm.

An opulent lunch was served at noon in the Royal Cliff's Chrysanthemum Palace with all kinds of exotic Asian dishes and lots of fruit at the end. I was introduced to other prof's as the new arrival from Canada and the United States and endured the ensuing small talk without pain. After lunch we all had a few hours off to enjoy the pool, followed by traditional Thai wrist tying of the students, the so called "Bai Sri" ceremony, followed by dinner entertainment until around ten o'clock.

A group of profs under the leadership of unrelenting Jeff was formed to explore the nightlife of Pattaya, an although I was tired and worn out, I decided to join them so as not to be seen as a boring loner. We went to Tony's Disco in South Pattaya, strolled along the walking street, and at midnight just about split, but Jeff insisted that he and I explore a famous disco that he had frequented with great success a year ago.

"When a girl takes you home from a disco," Jeff insisted, "it means she really likes and wants you."

"Okay, let's go," I replied.

We walked a couple of times up and down walking street but Jeff could not locate his favorite hangout, "Marine Disco", until alas! there it was. We went up the escalator and entered a large dark hall with deafening music and a beat that resonated in my chest. I didn't like it but said nothing. Jeff got beer for us and then started checking out the girls at the various tables.

I was standing on the sideline sipping on a Heineken.

"Come on, I've found two young ones who are new to the business," Jeff came up to me then disappeared and emerged with one of them on the dance floor, gesticulating wildly to the other and me to join them on the dance floor. The other girl, who I hadn't noticed before, emerged out of the darkness and I followed. Jeff started hopping and bopping holding his new acquaintance, while the other girl and I were standing next to them. Then I looked at her for the first time.

I looked at her pretty face, long black hair, full lips, high cheekbones and ever so slightly slant eyes. She was not slim and slender but had strong shoulders proportionate to her size, was about 18 to 19 years old, I thought, about 165 centimeters tall with long legs wearing tight jeans and high heel sandals.

As I looked at her I felt like I was already in love with her which has never happened to me in my entire life before so quickly. She looked back at me with a faint Mona Lisa smile and as I saw her face closer, looking into her mellow eyes, I thought to myself, "I know this person." It had happened only a few times in my life before that I met an apparent stranger and felt instantly connected as if I knew the person, perhaps from prior lives that the Buddhist I am believes in.

We now stood face to face and I put my arm around her waist while she placed her hand and arm on my shoulder. We began to move back and forth to the music none of us in the mood to rock. She felt warm and soft around the waste, and I noticed that I was getting a hard on. We exchanged a few words, but she spoke no English, only "hello", "where you from", "what's your name".

I said, "Michael from Canada, and you?"

"Iuu."

"Iuu, how old are you?"

No answer. I was worried about getting involved with some under age girl as I didn't know what the legal age for short-term romance was in Thailand.

Jeff noticed that we were talking, came over and offered to help by first asking and then yelling:

"How old are you? Are you eighteen yet?"

He got only a consternated look back from Iuu, but no reply. After repeating his questions several times with increasing intensity, Jeff answered them himself:

"Okay, you are over eighteen. Okay."

We continued dancing and looking at each other for another five minutes, then I turned to Jeff:

"What are we waiting for? It's late? Why don't we make a move?"

It was agreed that we would take our new brides to the Royal Cliff for the night. We didn't even ask, I guess, but simply walked hand in hand downstairs to Walking Street and then took one of the mini buses on Beach Road up to the Royal Cliff.

A bookstore was still open and Jeff suggested that I buy a dictionary.

"It's no fun if you can't communicate," he insisted.

I sloughed it off, saying: "It's okay, we'll let our hands do the talking."

"We have to be careful at the hotel," said Jeff, "that no one sees us because we're supposed to behave, you know."

I said nothing but kept smiling at Iuu who was squeezing my hand and smiling back at me, perhaps understanding the situation but, I was quite sure, none of the words. I noticed that the palm of her hand was slightly wet, indicating that she was nervous. Jeff was right, I thought, she was obviously new to the Pattaya night scene and still shy. What a night this will be, I thought, after nine years without a woman. Romantic feelings started rising from my treasure into my head, and I looked at Iuu again feeling happy. She was so young, so beautiful, and delicate. What a gift, I thought to myself.

I led the way into the hotel, looked around and noticed a few people sitting on a couch around a table, motioning to Iuu to stop walking. She froze instantly. Then the all-clear sign, and we rushed to the elevator and disappeared in our rooms each with his girl for a night of togetherness.

Iuu smiled at me as she checked out the luxurious room while I thought it would be a bad move to get right down to business.

Iuu started arranging my clothes, putting shirts on the hanger and hanging them up in the closet, and generally making a little order that I thought to myself, what a lovely gesture, my wife wouldn't have even done that for me, my German or my Canadian one that is.

"Have a nice bath, Iuu, and relax, " I suggested to her to calm her and make her feel comfortable and at home.

I let the water into the bathtub, and five minutes later she was splashing about with delight while I turned on the TV and contemplated the things that were to transpire.

I was tired, quite tired, I thought, but the promise of love and pleasure, I was not going to let it slip through my hands. So I pulled myself together, took off my clothes and put on the comfortable housecoat provided by the hotel.

About fifteen minutes later, Iuu emerged from the bathroom, her head and body wrapped in a white towel.

What a sight, I thought to myself. My "Orchid Girl". Smooth almond skin, beautiful face and eyes, came towards me and sat by my side. We hugged briefly, then it was my turn to take my shower.

When I was done I found her sitting on the balcony marveling at the lights of Pattaya below and the dark ocean in the distance with many brightly lit fishing vessels, a very romantic sight. I sat down beside her. We looked at each other, smiling slightly, without saying a word. I was happy, and in love I thought, and if she wasn't also, she was putting on a very good act.

This is beautiful, so beautiful, I thought to myself, sex or no sex, I don't care. I was afraid it might happen to me again, being too much in love suppressed my potency, but not this time.

We stretched out on the bed together and as I tried to enter her she was not open. We gave up and laughed about our dilemma.

She went back to the bathroom, and minutes later we did it together, me on top of her, her on top of me, until I felt I was released.

We had a drink from the room bar, watched a little TV together, and at around 2 a.m. went to bed, but however tired I was I couldn't sleep, neither could she. I held her in my arms, stroking her hair gently with my hands, and kissing her on the forehead. She responded by tapping her fingers on my back and shoulders, saying: "Sleep, sleep, sleep...."

We engaged in simple conversation.

She seemed to want to know if I was married, how many children (she said "babees") I had. I replied by holding up four fingers.

She tried to explain where her parents lived saying words like "Kang", "Udon", and such other sounds that meant nothing to me.

I tried to explain that I was from Canada pointing to what I thought she would understand is the north, being a very big country. She seemed to understand by agreeing, but I was certain that she did not. It didn't matter, anyway.

We must have fallen asleep in each other's arms for an hour or two when it got light outside. I checked the time. It was only six o'clock in the morning. I looked at her again beginning to feel that I was in love with Iuu. After a good night's rest I normally awake with a hard on, but not this time. I wasn't in the mood for sex and believed neither was she. Iuu explained to me that her girl friend who went with Jeff had her room key. I called Jeff on the house phone, mistakenly calling him Jim.

"If you call me Jim again, I won't talk to you anymore", he barked. "What do you want?"

I explained and a couple minutes later the key was slid under our door.

Iuu made herself ready to go home, and a little sad about our parting, I dressed to accompany her to see her off.

Just before she was ready to leave I reached for the hotel stationary and a pen and asked her to write down her name and address. She understood and did so in beautifully drawn Thai letters saying, in their translation that I obtained from an ABAC student the following day:

Iuu LOVES Michael
Watcharapon [last name omitted]
Muban Nonglard
Tambon Nongmek
Amphur Nonghan
Province Udon Thani 40330

Before we left the room, I grabbed all of the baht notes I had in my wallet, 1,500 baht in all, put them in an envelope and gave it to her.

"Thank you," she said in English, and put the envelope away without opening it.

It was already quite warm outside on this Sunday morning, 27th May 2001. I paid the limo outside and rode with Iuu to the gate of the Royal Cliff. She smiled at me and on parting gave me a kiss on the mouth and waved good-by as the limo pulled away. Thai's don't kiss, I had read, so this was something extra just for me, I thought.

I went back to the hotel room and felt utterly empty and lonely inside, missing her. I felt a choke and lump in my throat, a little sick in my stomach, and my heart began to hurt. My Orchid Girl had left. I was without my New Love. Would I ever see her again? May be, I thought, at the end of my term I could travel to her village and look for her, may be even find her, if she wanted me. I wasn't sure.

I went to the swimming pool for a dip and met Jeff splashing about.

"How did you like it," he inquired with a grin on his face.

"I love her," I replied.

"What's her name?"

"Iuu," I replied, "nineteen years old."

"How much money did you give her?"

"One thousand five hundred bath," I remarked.

Jeff exploded: "What? Fifteen hundred bath? You crazy or something?" he yelled.

"I said I love her. If I had had more on me, I would have given that to her, too."

"You do gooders spoil it for all the rest of us. I never pay more than five hundred bath. I gave her six hundred. Now I have to give my girl more too. I got her number. I'm going to meet her again. Listen, pal. I'm never going to go out with you again. That's it. That's it."

Jeff was furious. I didn't care. What a cheap guy I thought to myself. He made a couple of other remarks that I didn't care to hear, and than flipped onto his back on top of the water, and, floating, proclaimed with self-satisfaction:

"This is living! This is living!"

Jeff was happy again.

The rest of the day, including breakfast and the trip back to Bangkok was spent in sweet memory but otherwise utter misery. Every minute, every second, I could only think of Iuu, where she might be, what she might do, how young she was, just a teenager out of high school, and I a middle-aged man and a bit more. Hopeless, I thought. No hope whatsoever for a future. I had never had sex in my life with a woman I didn't love. I could count my encounters on both hands. Problem, Michael, problem, I thought. Why oh why can't you just enjoy the fun and move on with your life? I felt both blessed by her presence and cursed by her absence. Three more months of agony, I thought, and then a glimmer of hope may be, may be not. I felt happily unhappy.

This is Thailand! This very same thing happens every year to thousands of much younger farangs (foreigners) than I, and many middle-aged men, who, leaving their brains at the airport, plunge into a new life with a young Thai woman trying, and many times successfully so, at getting their youth back. Some take their new brides home to their country, others start a new life in Thailand. Was I going to be one of them? I doubted it that I could do it with Iuu who would be the only one for me, given our age difference, but we will see.

Chapter 3
Udon Thani

On Monday the following day after our night together at the Royal Cliff Beach Resort in Pattaya, being back in Bangkok, I realized that I had made a mistake of not connecting better with "Iuu" by getting her address and phone number in Pattaya.

I went to the bus station in Ekkamai and took the bus to Pattaya, checked into a cheap but clean hotel, Hotel Sureena on Soi Post Office, and went to the Marine Disco at around nine in the evening waiting for Iuu to reappear.

I waited in vain for two nights until two o'clock in the morning. The waiters became friendly with me and pointed out any number of girls who would be glad to be my brides for the night.

"Take this one. Take that one." And pointing to an obviously underage girl who motioned customers to patron the establishment, he added: "She fucks."

Undercover police checked me out inquiring about what I was doing sitting at the same table for hours on end.

"Okay, waiting for lady," they determined and left me alone.

During the day the manager of the hotel, Mrs. Long, an attractive thirty year old, talked to me to understand my story.

I asked her a pointed question:

"What is the acceptable age difference between a man like myself and a young woman."

"Marry an eighteen year-old," she replied without hesitation.

"Really," I asked with surprise, "I can marry a young girl like this?"

"No problem," she replied. "This is Thailand."

I started drafting post cards to Iuu in her village knowing she would not read them until she returned home, who knows when.

Mrs. Long helped me by correcting my Thai.

I copied simple sentences from the book like "The weather is nice today." "How are you feeling." "What food do you like?"

always ending with "I love you very much and want to marry you." Then I posted them stating my return address and telephone number.

On the third day I returned to Bangkok depressed and a lot less hopeful.

I went to the university library and took out books on Isan, and maps looking for Nonglard, for Nonghan, Nongmek. Udon Thani was easy to find.

I asked a student to translate Iuu's note for me. I asked him, is Watcharapon a boy's or a girl's name.

"A boy's name," he answered with a funny smile on his face.

"No, must be a girl," I protested.

He looked at the original Thai version and corrected himself with relief.

"Oh, a girl's name, of course. In her Thai writing it's Watcharaporn not ...pon."

"Thank you," I said with relief.

Eventually, using a search engine for Thai postal codes, I learned that the postal code 41133 she had given me matched Nonghan in the Province of Udon Thani.

On Sunday afternoon, June 3rd, I couldn't stand it anymore and decided on a bold strategy to find Iuu, and put it into action right away by calling Thai Airways and making a reservation for the Monday morning flight to Udon Thani, returning on Thursday evening, June 7th. I had five days off, as my teaching days were Friday and Sunday.

I got up at five, took a taxi to Bangkok's Don Muang International Airport at six, and boarded the eight o'clock flight to Udon Thani arriving at nine. In the limo to the city I met a lady who said she was taking the bus that went through Nonglard. I should simply follow her.

I saw the countryside was primitive but nice. Trees lined the highway. The bus stopped in the Amphur Nonghan, a small regional town with a busy market, and fifteen minutes later I stepped off the bus on the highway just outside the village of Nonglard.

It had been raining and the potholes on the street I was entering were full of water. The houses were wooden with cracks in the walls to allow ventilation. There were chicken and ducks running about, banana and coconut trees in the yards.

As I entered the village, a young man got up from under the houses where people squatted and children were playing. He approached me and asked something I couldn't understand, so I showed him the note that Iuu had written with her name and address in Thai.

He looked at it, smiled back at me, and said something that I would think meant, "You are looking for Iuu?"

I said, "krap", which meant so much as yes, I do.

He took me by the hand and walked me down the street towards the center of the village, stopping at each house and answering the curious questions from the squatting villagers, mentioning the word "Iuu" and laughing.

I felt awkward. I knew that I should not be doing this, a middle-aged man in love, running after a young nineteen year-old teenager. I tried to look my best, smiling as much as I could at any occasion. But then again, Mrs. Long had encouraged me, so why not move ahead?

We arrived at a clean house with a small also clean courtyard and a few shrubs, and the young man pointed at it nodding his head. A couple of folks were squatting underneath the neighbor's house, more people arrived, and a lot of children, about 30 all in all, looking at me in amusement and talking amongst each other with excitement.

The house that was shown to me was locked, no one in it. My heart sank.

A young woman approached with a baby on her arm looking surprisingly similar to Iuu that for a moment I thought to myself:

"Have I forgotten what Iuu looks like? Is this the one?"

I handed her the present. Just a book and a small bracelet wrapped in a box with Iuu's name on it. She took it smiling, but the villagers upon reading and exclaiming the name "Iuu" ripped it out of her hands and gave it back to me.

This went on for about fifteen minutes when a thirty year-old woman appeared who asserted that she was Iuu's sister. My optimism rose.

"You want to marry Iuu?" she asked.

The mail in Thailand is obviously faster than I had expected of a somewhat Third World country. The post cards I had sent from Pattaya had already arrived and been read, the news spreading fast in a northeast village that is somewhat cut off from the faster pace of the more industrialized south. In fact, the mail in Thailand is quite expeditious. Thailand Post had asked the Canadians to rebuild the country's mail system, and they had done a good job.

"Yes," I replied wondering at my own determination, "I have come to ask Iuu to marry me."

The sister who actually turned out to be a cousin by the name of Nog, translated her question and my reply into Isan and the community surrounding me took notice with approval, it seemed.

Nog led me to her house which had a public pay phone and said she would make a couple of inquiries to find out where Iuu was. I emptied my wallet and produced all the coin I had, and flashed a couple of bills that were changed into coins by the village shopkeeper across the street.

Exited discussions over the telephone went on endlessly, it seemed. After about thirty minutes I got the news:

"A family member will contact Iuu to hear what she has to say. Come again tomorrow, and we will tell you. No, better yet, come in two days and then you know what is happening," said Nog. "May be you are lucky, may be not lucky."

"I can go back to Udon Thani and stay at a hotel," I replied.

"Yes," said Nog, "but no fucking if Iuu is coming, you know?"

"No, no, I said. Absolutely not. I am not doing that!" I confirmed.

"Okay, when you are at the hotel, call me so I have your number, and give me the hotel room number also."

I stayed another few minutes, thanking Nog kindly for her help and assistance, flung my travel bag over my shoulder, and was driven back to the bus stop on the back of a motorcycle. As we passed the houses, the news of where I was going and what was to happen, was shared with the squatters under the houses. It was some event for the village, perhaps the event of the day: Ferang coming to their village in person to ask for Iuu's hand in wedlock. Wow and laughter.

I found a hotel near the old bus stop and called Nog to give her the telephone and room number. Nog, who spoke surprisingly clear English, reminded me to remain abstinent, to relax and wait until she called me again, hopefully the next morning. I agreed and thanked her profusely.

I felt no longer lonely and forsaken, but the feeling that took over now was fear, a happy fear of seeing Iuu again, and perhaps, oh well, only perhaps, taking her home with me. But look at me, what the hell was I doing? Was this just another game life plaid on me, or I myself on life?

The night went by and at around ten o'clock in the morning the maid knocked on my door saying "telephone". I rushed downstairs to the office and picked up the receiver.

"This is Nog. How are you today?"

"I'm fine, thank you you, I'm fine. Yes?"

And then Nog spoke the words that I will never forget in my life, and I feel a lump in my throat as I write these words:

"Iuu is taking the bus tonight and will be in Nonglard tomorrow morning. So you can come at around nine, okay?"

"Thank you, oh, thank you so much, Nog. You are a real help and a very nice lady. Thank you. I will be there at nine in the morning."

I ran up the stairs into my room, closed the door and fell on the bed, crying for joy. I didn't want to stop, I just cried on and on. It was heavenly, Iuu will come. But will she say "yes", or is she coming home anyway?

The happy thoughts prevailed all through the night and in the morning I woke with the break of day at five-thirty. I ate a light breakfast and went back into my room not wanting to be disturbed by the busy activities of the city.

I went to the bus station and now knowing my way around, took the eight o'clock bus to Nonglard, arriving at about nine.

The villagers welcomed me as they did two days before with curious observations and lots of talking amongst themselves. Young children practiced their English by shouting:

"Hello! Hello"

"Hello," I replied, "how are you?"

They replied: "What's your name? Where you come from?"

"My name is Michael. I come from Canada."

"Hah, hah, hah..." was their reply making fun out of any situation and enjoying it.

The village people of Isan don't have much, it seems, but they surely have each other and their fun and good natured humor. They are the best people of Thailand, I have heard it said many times by foreigners, and they certainly are the ones that I have learned to love through Iuu.

There was already a fairly large gathering in front of Iuu's house when I arrived. I was welcomed warmly, was asked to sit down with the people in front of Iuu's house and offered the sign of welcome, a glass of cold water that I accepted and downed in a minute. It had been raining during the night, but it was still warm at around thirty degrees centigrade, I guessed.

I was told that Iuu was inside washing herself.

Ten minutes went by, fifteen, and twenty that seemed like hours. Then the door opened and she came out as beautiful as she was with a big smile on her face.

I rushed forward, put my arms around her waist and lifted her up. Then we hugged briefly and sat down together. There was a murmur of applause from the village gatherers, and Iuu turned to them and started talking and answering questions upon questions.

Iuu introduced me to her friends and cousins, and finally to grandmother, a wrinkled but smiley and forthright old lady in her seventies. Grandmother *swadeed* me courteously. I *swadeed* her back. Her name was *Yai-Ob*, "yai" meaning old. We liked each other from the start.

I could and did not take my eyes off of Iuu, and she looked at me, too, but kept her cool about herself, smiling and saying a few words in broken English.

Then Nog arrived and we took a motor tricycle to a nearby restaurant at a fish pond for an early lunch. Iuu was quite hungry. I was told that father and mother would arrive the following day. Oha, I thought, getting serious, may be wedding bells ringing. I was the happiest I had been in ten years.

We spent the afternoon walking around the village. Iuu was greeted warmly and spent half an hour or longer at each house. I did not understand a word, but knew exactly what the conversation was all about. The people's looks inspected me from top to bottom, smiling warmly at me and back at Iuu. Some food and water was offered, always.

At night, Iuu and I bedded down next to grandmother on the concrete floor of the living room. I had understood from Nog that I could not have sex with Iuu in her father's and mother's house, so I lay still next to Iuu. Eventually, grandmother seemed to have fallen asleep when Iuu knocked me ever so lightly with her elbow, motioning me to go upstairs with her. I put my finger on my lips and whispered "hush", but to no avail. A minute later she started egging me on again until I got the message and quietly followed her upstairs into her room.

There a big bed made out of mattresses was spread out on the floor with two pillows and blankets. Iuu pulled me down to her, and we began to celebrate our first night together in her house where she had grown up as a child and into which she now welcomed me with her strong arms, sweet lips, and ever so smooth and tender body. I was on cloud nine and in fairyland.

Eventually, the rain came, a downpour, and pounded on the metal roof that formed the ceiling, drowning out all sounds and noises that we might have made loving each other in a wild ride of joy and happiness into the night until we sank into each other's arms and just slept.

Chapter 4
Our Wedding Day

One may debate about what was our wedding day. According to Mahayana Buddhism in which I was trained in Vancouver for three years prior to arriving in Thailand, it is the day of the first sexual union, which would have been the night from May 26th to 27th of 2001. But that would have meant, "Iuu" would have been married three or four times before she wed me so that this first wedding day is debatable.

On the day following Iuu's arrival in Nonglard, on June 7th, 2001, her mother and father arrived from Klang, Province of Rayong, where they were living and working.

Father was the only one who could have been reached by telephone when Nog called around. He was told that a farang was waiting in Nonglard to marry Iuu. He rushed to Pattaya about an hour and a half away by bus, found Iuu and told her to go to Nonglard and take a chance to see for herself.

Iuu, hearing my name, had agreed and father returned by bus to Klang to travel to Nonglard with his wife the following day. They didn't want me to wait in my hotel room in Udon Thani for more than two days. Therefore the rush. All of this was related to me much later by Iuu.

Mother and father, taking the night bus, arrived about two hours after Iuu and I had gotten up the following morning from what I for myself consider to be our wedding night. According to my understanding of the Mahayana Buddhist teachings, our wedding days are both June 6th and 7th of June, 2001.

It was a great moment coupled with anxiety and expectations to meet mother, Tang-On, then age 41, and father, Bungkert, age 43, in the humble surroundings of their house in Nonglard. Two people who I had heard and believed had the power of decision whether or not I, about ten years their senior, could marry their daughter, my love and my one and only Iuu, age 19.

I saw Bungkert approach with a faint smile and a somewhat high pitched but sympathetic voice, stretching out his hand to me and greeting me with a warm "hello." Tang-On swadeed courteously, and kept behind Bungkert when he sat down with me in the living room beginning the "interrogation".

Where are you from, how old are you, are you married?

"No, I am not married, I am divorced from my wife, so I am single."

We were surrounded by a crowd of cousins and neighbors listening in. When Bungkert heard "single", he announced it in Isan to all of the onlookers.

"He is single, not married," meaning that Iuu would be a first wife not a mistress. He obviously liked that because it meant better support, an inheritance, and the children would be legitimate with full rights, too. It appears, though, that he would have also accepted if Iuu was to be my mistress but well taken care of.

He inquired of my status, my work, income, and plans I had to secure Iuu's future. I had expected these questions and announced that I was thinking of buying land for Iuu to start a macadamia nut farm in Nonglard or surroundings as an investment, or whatever else I could find in the future. I said that my income was very good for Thai standards, and, finally, I said that I truly loved Iuu and wanted her to be my wife to hold and to cherish… and so on.

After talking like this to each other for about fifteen minutes, mother Tang-On, looking over Bungkert's shoulder and smiling at me all the time, I knew that I had passed the test when Bungkert announced:

"Now I want cigarettes and beer!"

At that point, Iuu went into action and asked me for money to buy the beer, cigarettes, and food to prepare a great meal for all of us and the attending cousins and neighbors.

This was all of the worldly wedding ceremony Iuu and I have had to this day. I had to teach the following morning, and to Bungkert's disappointment had to return by airplane to Bangkok the same night. The money I gave Iuu, not knowing what anything cost, was too small so that she had to return again asking for more.

A full-blown wedding ceremony costs around 40,000 to 80,000 baht. The dowry paid in cash is exposed for inspection by the guests although it may be inflated because parts of may be put up for show and refunded to the bridegroom who is paying it after the ceremony is over just to maintain face.

For a village wedding ceremony, large amounts of Isan whisky called "Laokhao" made from rice, and beer, flow, huge amounts of food are consumed, music is played, maybe even videos shown from enormous screens and load speakers by commercial providers, and the road is blocked off. This was not the case at all at Iuu's and my spontaneous surprise wedding, which therefore is a missing piece of perfection in our union.

Iuu said that we will have the wedding later when our house has been built.

In the afternoon, Iuu, her mother and an aunt, led me to the local temple, the "Wat", where the monk, the "Prah", blessed our marriage in a small ceremony right in front of him while we were kneeling down and making our vows. First he talked to us, asking me the standard question in passable English where I came from and what I was doing in Thailand, then nodding. Then he turned to Iuu and conversed with her in Isan or Thai. I did not notice the difference yet, having been in Thailand for only a month. He prayed with us for a while, then wrist-tied both of us, as did many cousins, aunts, uncles, and neighbors, and, of course, Iuu's parents.

Iuu had told me before, to give the Prah some money for his service, and having no smaller bill, I put a five-hundred baht note into his hand.

The Prah looked at it in amazement, and started the praying ceremony all over again. Iuu said later, twenty or fifty baht is what most people give.

At around four in the afternoon, the shopkeeper arrived in his Toyota pickup truck, and drove Iuu and me sitting in the back, mother and aunt sitting on the loading deck in the back, to the Udon Thani airport. We had to settle a small loan that mother had received from the shopkeeper to afford the trip to Nonglard (I don't understand the transaction).

Arriving or parting in Isan is made without any ritual. I have never seen Iuu say hello to her parents or embracing them when she arrived, or say good-by or anything when she parted. She simply arrived as if she had never left, or parted as if she wasn't going anywhere.

For those Westerners who dislike emotional and tearful good-bys the Thai style would be a welcome new way; for those who do, the Isan way seems cold and remote, but it isn't. The family is so strongly connected, I believe, that they can easily do without the Western rituals by simply accepting the raw reality as it is.

The same with divorce, I have learned from Iuu. Every feeling, any memory, any artifact, are simply removed or sold off for money, instantly. There's nothing left, no photo, not even a memory which is suppressed until it fades into nothingness. Brutal, it seems in the minds of the romantic Westerns. Real, in the minds of the people of Isan, I guess.

Isan people by their nature do not seem to be romantic. I have never seen Iuu's mother and father caress or be tender with each other, although Iuu, but only in private, is always creating romance in our marriage whenever she can. When I lie down to take a rest, she removes all obstacles placed on the bed and lies down with me embracing me. She kisses me when I sit in front of the computer, and reads my mind and rejoices if sex is on my mind, offering herself always, never holding back or even refusing.

I had never known the honesty, sincerity and sheer happiness and pleasure that Iuu would create in our marriage.

The flight from Udon Thani to Bangkok was Iuu's first, ever. She cuddling beside me under a blanket, pretending that she was sleeping but she later admitted she did it to hide her fear of flying.

We arrived in about and hour, and one hour later we were in our new home together, married as husband and wife. It took me a while to realize that this was reality, that I had my Orchid Girl beside me in my studio room who I had fallen in love with at first sight, seemed to have lost, and then found, and that Iuu had actually agreed to marry and move in with me without any hesitation whatsoever.

Iuu later confided in me that she had consulted her parents, who agreed to the marriage, and her grandmother who approved, saying: "He's handsome."

The age factor that troubled me was never put in issue, Iuu said. Only father had asked me how old I was, fifty-one, or sixty-one. It didn't matter.

As a young girl Iuu said she had prayed to her Prah: "Please give me a farang in marriage." And she told me later: "Older is okay."

When I surfaced in her life, being the first farang she went to bed with, it seemed to Iuu that her prayers had been heard and answered. She was well prepared, therefore in her quick and affirmative response of saying "yes" and marrying me.

In the morning I introduced Iuu to my Dean in the Graduate School of Business at ABAC, Brother Vinai, to ask his permission for living together with Iuu in our studio room at Queens Tower. He approved.

Then he interviewed Iuu in Thai for a good fifteen minutes and answered my question how old Iuu was because I still wasn't sure as I could not read her Thai I.D. card:

"She is nineteen, was born on September 8, 1981. There's a rule that she must be twenty before you can live together, but she'll be twenty in a short while, so that is okay."

In answer to my question how to convert the Buddhist calendar to the Christian, he replied: "You subtract 543 years."

Brother Vinai also said that my intentions to enroll Iuu in school and provide her with an education would be useless. He said she does not want to study, so that I should simply enjoy her and not bother which would only give us problems. I decided to disprove him, but he remained at least partially right most of the time.

Then Brother Vinai called the guards at Queen's Tower who had made a fuss the night before about letting Iuu into the building, that she was cleared. When we returned to our room, the guards bowed to us and offered their apologies.

Chapter 5
First Year at ABAC

The news of our marriage so soon after my arrival in Thailand spread quickly among the faculty. Colleagues smiled at me and said I looked a lot more relaxed and handsome that when I had first arrived a month ago.

Jeff came back a week later. I bumped into him at the lake while walking home from my office. In his usual upbeat mood, he asked:

"How's it going. Have you had any contact with your girl?"

"She's here," I replied.

"WHAT, she is HERE?" he exclaimed.

"I married her." I said calmly.

"WHAT, you MARRIED her?" He was now totally flabbergasted.

"Yes, I married her. We love each other," I explained. "I just fell in love."

"WOW. Are you SURE you know what you are doing? WOW, what a SURPRISE."

A couple days later I met Jeff again. He had seen his girl of the particular evening, "Iuu's" friend Lung, again who is also from Nonglard but a few years older than Iuu and had worked in Pattaya for a couple of years.

Jeff said that every one of her friends knew that Iuu had married a farang after working in Pattaya for only three weeks. The goal of many a beer bar girl from Isan – and ninety percent of them come from the northeast – is to marry a farang with money so that they can stop working and provide for their families back home. Iuu had already made it in very short order.

My first formal duty, I felt, was to get my marriage to Iuu legalized by registering at the Amphur, the Government District Office. Without official marriage certificate, I felt, the Canadian Embassy would not issue Iuu a visa to travel home with me if and when my teaching term at ABAC expired. I was deeply troubled by the prospect that I might have to leave my young wife behind at the end of my teaching term only two and half months away.

As a first step toward registration of our marriage, the Canadian Embassy in Bangkok had to confirm that I was eligible. After producing my prior divorce papers, they obliged. The certificate issued by the embassy had to be translated into Thai and confirmed by the Consular Services of the Foreign Ministry. An agency looked after that for a thousand baht fee.

Iuu was not of legal age, yet, being only nineteen so that her parents' consent was required. I suggested that now that we had the papers we could simply wait three months until her birthday on September 8th, 2001, and spare the extra trip. But Iuu said she wanted to be lawfully married now, and hearing it from her made me happy.

We took the bus to Klang and went with the parents to the local Amphur. The officers refused us and said we would have to do it in either Pattaya or Bangkok where the Amphurs were equipped for registering marriages between a Thai and a foreigner, they were not.

Father and mother, Iuu and I took the bus to Bangkok the same evening, where I put the parents up at the ABAC hotel in a separate room. The next morning, after failing once, we located the right Amphur in Buengkum, a suburb east of the City of Bangkok, and registered our marriage within an hour.

The marriage registration in substance involved a confirmation and an undertaking on my part that I had the income or means to care for my wife at all times, which Iuu accepted with her signature, and once signed and witnesses by her parents as well, who thereby also consented because Iuu was legally underage, the official certificate was issued.

Father and mother returned to Klang while Iuu and I celebrated at home. Now we were legally married. We were both very happy at the prospect of being bonded for life.

Our studio room on the 12th floor of Queen's Tower at ABAC, also known as "ABAC Hotel", was perfect for a newly wed couple such as ourselves. It had an area of about 50 square meters with a high 10-foot ceiling, including the wash room, a balcony, and a fantastic view of the city's skyline. It was facing west so that we couldn't be awakened by the glaring sunlight in the mornings. Instead, we were presented almost every day with gorgeous tropical sunset. The room was large enough for two to be close to each other at all times, was comfortable enough for sleeping, watching TV, or doing work on the computer.

It didn't matter to Iuu that we didn't have a kitchen. Iuu bought an electric wok and a rice cooker, placed a plastic table cover on the floor, hunkered down in the typical Isan squatting position, chopping away at vegetables and meat, and had a meal ready in about ten minutes' time. I was amazed at her skills of adapting to her new situation. She would wash the dishes in the bathroom sink, which got plugged very quickly, but we had a plunger to clear it daily.

We had a coffee machine, a toaster, and lots of spices and dry food in the drawers of her dresser. The household in our small but livable home was complete. The best thing about was that it was free of rent and charges.

Iuu asked me from time to time where we would move when the baby comes. There were many town houses for rent around ABAC, I replied, and we would simply move into one. She answered if the baby came, she would have it in Isan, spending the last months of her pregnancy in Nonglard. She really wanted a baby, and I rejoiced at the thought, but we didn't get lucky as her period was very irregular and the treatment at Ramkhamhaeng Hospital she took for one month did not seem to work. She felt depressed but said it wouldn't worry her, but I think it did.

Iuu spent the hours from 8:30 to 10:30 at night glued to the TV, watching the popular Thai drama show on ITV's Channel 3. I noticed that the whole family in Nonglard, if not the village, did the same. She said that she had no Thai friend so that the TV was her substitute. Sometimes, I felt she was acting out the scenes in our marriage relationship, especially later when she started screaming at me from time to time when she was angry.

I liked to walk down the streets and alleys with Iuu hand in hand. Sometimes Iuu objected saying that now, since she was Madam, people would think of her as being my mistress. Only mistresses would hold hands and smooch their short-time lovers in public. And then she said the famous words that she spoke so often:

"Michael, you will have me a long time."

I always took great comfort in hearing her promise when she said it, time and again, and she knew very well that I did. From time to time the thought arose in me, what would she do if in twenty years' time I would be over the hill while she was still in her forties and still desirous of love and romance. We even talked about it sometimes. I insisted that longevity ran in my family, that my mother was still very active into her mid-eighties at which time Iuu would be in her fifties. I thought we will have no problem with our age difference, as fifty year-old women in Isan seemed rather old and resigned to their fate. Staying active and keeping fit by thinking young, I thought I can be her true partner for several more decades. After all, the famous Spanish painter, Pablo Picasso, had fathered a child with his housemaid when he was in his nineties.

The next obstacle was to obtain a passport, but the passport should show my name not her maiden name.

Again we traveled to Nonglard and went to the local Amphur in Nonghan to get the proper certificate. It took two days and a small amount of tea money to expedite the services. Iuu was now Watcharaporn Schemmann and started practicing to write her new name.

Next, we applied for a Canadian visitor's visa for Iuu which is generally not easy to obtain. After a little bit of wrangling, the Thai official working at the embassy granted Iuu an eighteen-month multiple entry visa. I sighed a sigh of relief, and Iuu was proud to have the visa in her passport.

Iuu and I were exchanging our life stories. She said she had been married before. I was both surprised and interested.

"He came by my house every day, brought me presents and talked nice", she said.

"Who is 'he'?" I asked.

"A forty-some year old man from the neighboring village of Bang Chiang."

"How did you meet him," I asked.

"His sister lives in Nonglard. He came to visit his sister and one day he noticed me. I was laughing at girls who married older men. Never do that. Never laugh at people. Say nothing. All of a sudden I got an older man myself."

"Was he nice, handsome, had money and all that?" I inquired.

"He was short and stocky and not really nice, but had a small business, an ice vending business and a car. He was stingy ("keenee-ow"), never bought me any food saying I should have eaten at home, and this. One day he was boxing me and I boxed him back. Then I kicked him out of the house and he had to return living in his village. He cried and wanted to come back, but I said no, no way. So I finished him."

"How old were you, Iuu, when you married the first time," I asked.

"We married on my eighteenth birthday," she replied. "I made myself beautiful, and he paid for a big wedding party that cost about 10,000 baht and gave me a gold necklace and paid 50,000 baht cash to mother. About seventy thousand baht in all. After I finished him, he wanted his money back and brought the

mayor, Sompon, to negotiate. Sompon is a cousin of my grandmother. I said, no, no money back because he fucked me." She laughed at me with a victorious smile as she said it. Iuu, I had noticed, first and foremost wants to think of herself as a winner.

"So that was only a year and a half ago."

"Yes," she replied.

"Did you love him, or why did you marry him?" I inquired.

"No I didn't love him. I married him because I thought it was the right thing to do. Mother needed the money to settle some debts."

"You saved your virginity for him all these years, didn't you. Did you at least enjoy your wedding night?"

"No, I didn't enjoy it at all because I didn't love him," Iuu replied with an ever so slight sigh in her voice.

"What did you do with the gold necklace?" I wondered.

"I sold it. I kept nothing from him. Not even a memory like he never existed. Finished is finished." She said in a resolute way. She was Khmer, I realized, the people from the former capital city of Angkor in Cambodia who had dominated Isan for many centuries. They are the fighting kind who kill mercilessly, but are also the most seductive when they love. I had some troublesome thoughts about being "finished" by Iuu, but suppressed them.

"What's his name and where is he now. Did he remarry?" I asked.

"I don't know and I don't care," said Iuu getting a little emotional. "When its finished it's finished. Up to him what he wants to do. Don't ask me these questions. I don't know and I don't care." Full stop, I thought. Wow, a flipside of my beautiful adorable, tender and young Isan wife that I hadn't expected.

"But you could have parted as friends," I insisted playing the game. "After all you were married at one point in time."

"Married, no I never really married him. Only a house marriage, but not registered at the Amphur." Now she was teaching me.

And then she added what sounded like a threat, almost:

"If you ever box me, that will be the end. I will move out and never, never come back," she said with a bit of fire in her eyes.

The custom in Isan, and perhaps the rest of Thailand, is that the man pays a dowry to the mother that is negotiated by the parents, and then moves into the bride's house as a matter of right, making her home his. This stocky older guy, probably without a neck, moved right into Iuu's bedroom that was hers alone since childhood, and then even became bossy, if I could believe Iuu's story. I could see how this situation very quickly got out of hand, Iuu being the number one person in her family who was smart, determined, and told everyone what to do, and how. I had realized on the first day I reunited with her in Nonglard how she was instantly the boss of the family, and everyone listened and obeyed her.

"What about children, you could have gotten pregnant easily in three month."

"I took the pill because I didn't want to have a baby from a man I didn't love," she replied.

"Are you taking the pill now, Iuu," I pressed on. "I don't see you do or have any. Just asking."

Then she came on over to me, realizing the game I was playing.

"I really want a baby with you. It will be beautiful, a 'lukueng'. I want a baby so much."

She kissed me and we hugged.

"Mother had to wait two years before she had me. Maybe I've got a problem, too."

Iuu's period was very irregular. It could be that she didn't have a period for two and a half months. One day we decided to go and seek medical advice at Ramkhamhaeng Hospital. The diagnosis was that she had a hormone disorder, had too much testosterone, and was somewhat obese, just a bit. The doctor gave her pills and after we returned for the second checkup, the ultrasound found that she had two large eggs ready for fertilization in two days. We had a twenty percent chance of having twins and were both ecstatic.

We took a brief vacation on Koh Samed and gave it our best. I remember on the way home, on the boat, I asked her not to sit too close to the noisy and heavily vibrating inboard diesel engine. She did oblige, but the babies never came. She said we should give up the treatment.

"Baby comes when it comes. Only costs money to go to the hospital," she reasoned.

I think it was a mistake. We should have continued because five times a twenty percent chance equals a hundred percent by way of the mathematical likelihood of the probabilities.

I suggested to Iuu that she might be a little bit Tom, a girl-boy, with a small foam of a mustache on her upper lips which I said I thought was absolutely sexy and a turn-on for me. She laughed and agreed.

I had noticed the way she drove the motorcycle, and did things like cooking, washing, or plane talking, showing mannerisms of a man rather than a woman. She did not mind me talking like this because she knew she was strong and wanted to be strong. She had broad shoulders, too, and in general the physique of a man. She had a hard time finding clothes that had to be XL to fit.

"When we go to Canada," I said, "you will not be a big person and can buy what you need. No problem."

I loved her so much that even if she had been a boy, I think I would have converted to become gay just to live with her. It was her persona that I had fallen in love with and married, not her sexual attributes, which were also quite strong and fabulous once she got going, except that she did not open easily and could not have any sex in the morning which I disliked because I always woke up with a hard on. She replied that any man who is potent wakes up with a hard on, otherwise he would be impotent. She had read or heard it somewhere, she said. If she noticed that I really wanted her, though, she would make herself open and give herself to me. She never ever refused me like my German and Canadian prior wives had on occasion, forcing me into submission by withholding supply. Not Iuu. She was most generous in every way and always followed the call of duty.

Noticing how much I was in love with her, that I admired and adored her, Iuu was certainly delighted. At the time, however, in small things at first, she attempted to take control of our day to day lives. Had I been a younger person of her own age and generation, I doubt that our marriage would have survived the first year, but being older and more experienced in marital affairs, I gently worked around her attempts so that she soon noticed that I was not going to adhere to her whims and wishes. It seems awkward that I don't remember any actual instances. Whenever she did something I did not approve of, I also forgave her instantly because I loved her so much, and did not keep anything in my memory.

Iuu let me kiss and hug her many times throughout the day without responding in a likewise manner. That came in year two, and in year three she had become the more active partner producing and seeking romance. She mentioned, and at first I didn't understand what she meant:

"At first there may be little love, but love comes when couples live together."

With hindsight, I realize, that she was referring to herself, not to "couples" in general.

Grandmother noticed that in the washroom in Nonglard we showered together, and that I actually soaped and rinsed my wife. She thought that was very unusual and mentioned it to Iuu's parents. Grandmother remarked many times:

"Michael loves you very, very much."

It pleased me to hear Iuu mention it, because it was absolutely true.

After she was single again having kicked her first husband out of the house, Iuu was recruited to work at Kimberley-Clark in Hat Yai making surgical gloves. She accepted and worked in this southern city near the Malaysian border for about eight months, she said. She was given only one week of vacation but the journey alone by bus took two full days each way. She returned one day late and was fired. The pay was a fabulous 7,000 baht per month, she said, including overtime. The factory provided the accommodation but she would have to feed herself. She disliked the city of Hat Yai because it was unsafe she said. The population was predominantly Muslim who sometimes burned the schools or clashed with the police in protest in order to obtain independence for the region from Thailand.

After a few months together, Iuu began complaining of headaches. If I gave her an aspirin tablet she would soon stretch out on our bed and fall asleep. I asked whether she had ever had headaches in her village, Nonglard. She said she didn't, so I suggested that she return home for a week to reconnect with her many cousins and friends. She was delighted, packed and took the overnight bus from Monchit home to Nonglard on the very same evening. Anything I suggested and that was agreed by her was always put into immediate action. I soon learned that this was the Isan way. Contemplation and checking out alternatives was only interpreted as reneging, not doing as one said.

I accompanied her by taxi to Monchit Northern Bus Terminal in Bangkok and saw her off. I called her the following day at the neighbor's house.

"It's raining so hard, I cannot hear you," she complained so that we gave up. I called an hour later and the rain had stopped. We talked nice and confirmed that we loved each other.

"I miss you, Michael. I will see you next week. Don't think too much. I'm fine."

Sleeping alone for the first time in months without Iuu felt awful. It actually hurt. After teaching the morning class the next day I went home to my room and thought to myself, "this is no good."

Out of curiosity, I made a call to Thai Airways. They had space on the six o'clock evening flight. It was now four in the afternoon. I quickly accepted, packed a bag, and jumped into a taxi at ABAC, obviously relieved that I was doing something to see my wife again and surprise her.

The flight touched down at Udon Thani airport on time. A limousine for the very high price of 800 baht took me to Nonglard and stopped in front of Iuu's house with the noisy diesel engine running. Instantly, Iuu appeared on the balcony to check what was happening, then recognized me and smiled. She rushed downstairs to the limo and we hugged, a long and intense hug it was and a sweet kiss on the mouth.

We went inside the house arm in arm. Now she knew how much I really loved her. Again I feel a lump in my throat as I write these lines. There was never a woman in my life like Iuu to whom, although she was not perfect in every sense of the meaning of the word, I felt so connected, devoted, bonded and who I just could not be without.

Grandmother, too, was happy to see me again and started talking at me with excitement in Isan. I could not understand a word but had some idea of what she might be saying: "So you love your wife so much that you can't even be without her for only a couple of days." Grandmother was all smiles.

Iuu's parents were still working and living in Klang on the Eastern Seabord near Rayong. They were not home.

Iuu asked whether I was hungry, and then started to whip up a meal in a couple of minutes. She was a great cook and enjoyed cooking for me.

Our second night in her room was deeply intimate and fulfilling. From time to time the rain drummed on the roof and ceiling. All through the night roosters were crying believing mistakenly that day was about to break. At six o'clock in the morning the whole village was on their feet, and grandmother cooked the sticky rice on the open fire right below our bedroom. Black smoke from the charcoal fire filled our room, so we had to get up to escape from it. I loved every bit of this very Isan way of life, knowing it was all an integral part of the life of my Great Love and wife, Iuu.

Being involved in education professionally at ABAC, I took an interest in Iuu's education as well. She had graduated from primary school in Nonglard after the mandatory six years, completing grade six when she was twelve years old. After that she worked in the rice paddies for planting in June, and during the harvest in November. In between she worked as a day laborer cutting sugar which made her grow into a strong woman. She basically missed the formative years in education when higher learning takes place such as math skills, geography, social studies, a foreign language. It was a pity, I thought, because she was smart and alert but without any knowledge required to get a well-paying job or run a successful business.

I started teaching her percent, then light algebra, and, of course, English. Because she had no idea where my country Canada was, or Europe, or any country other than Thailand. I bought a world map and put it over our bed. From time to time I would say to her:

"I'll give you one hundred baht if you find Mozambique for me."

"Sure," she said and climbed on the bed eagerly searching with her fingers for the name.

"I help you. It's part of Africa," I suggested.

"Africa," she repeated, "Africa, A-fri-ca…. Here is Africa! What am I looking for again? How do you spell?" she asked.

"M-O-Z-A-M-B-I-Q-U-E."

Her fingers returned to the map checking all over the continent from North to South but she couldn't find it. The suddenly an outburst:

"Here it is. I found it," she rejoiced, stretching out her curved hand at me saying: "Money, money, money, please!"

I gave it to her and she put it proudly away into her piggy bank.

"For baby," she said. "This money is for our baby."

She was so easy to love and we might have made love right afterwards just to celebrate our happiness.

Iuu joined the Thai Ministry of Education's informal education program, a kind of Adult Basic Education program, and graduated two years later with Mathayum 3, the equivalent of grade nine, and then enrolled in the Mathayum 6 program that would graduate her in March 2005 with the Thai equivalent of high school graduation. She went every Sunday for three hours, first by bus, and later taking our Ford Ranger pickup showing herself off proudly as a "Mia Farang", the wife of a foreigner, a European or North American white man.

Iuu soon rose to the position of number one in her class, was entrusted with collecting and maintaining the class funds, that, when she spent the money for her own use, I refunded to her so that she would not lose face.

One of the requirements that the school made on graduation was that she have a job. A barber shop lady by the name of "Geet" accepted her for training as a hair stylist and she went every day for a couple of hours learning to shampoo hair, and eventually, she said, would learn cutting, too. But it never came to that. Soon, Iuu would go to see Geet on a regular basis talking about this and that for hours on end. She would call me on her Nokia and say:

"I'm at Geet's. Can you pick me up when you are finished teaching?"

Or she would take the car and drive herself.

How Iuu learned to drive is another story by itself worth telling.

In April 2002, I rented a Suzuki Jeep to take her family to Nonglard for Songkran, the Thai New Year's festival. We picked up the parents in Klang, her brother Tiu and his cousin, and drove the nine hours over the mountains in Khao Yai National Park to Nonglard. We arrived at two o'clock at night, woke up the whole neighborhood and the women started cooking a hefty meal.

Isan, no question is a lot of fun if fun is wanted. There are few conventions. One can do whatever one feels like, and do so at any time of the day or night.

One day at our first Songkran vacation in Nonglard, I gave Iuu driving lessons that ended in a near disaster. She backed the car up into the highway, engine screaming, and wouldn't let go of the accelerator. Somehow I got her to stop by jerking out the emergency hand brake. We were lucky, traffic on the highway much traveled by trucks was light.

The next morning, I was still sleeping, Iuu came back into our room, said something to me and while she did removed the car keys from my pocket. Then she drove the whole neighborhood to the market in Nonghan, the district town. I didn't realize what had happened until I realized she was gone and the car and the keys were missing. An hour or so later, she returned triumphantly and handed me the car keys, saying nothing.

I didn't dare to make a fuss, either, because by now she had obviously proven to herself and me that she could drive. I wished I had been so tactful on other occasions when my temper had the best of me and Iuu lost face and suffered, keeping her emotions deeply buried inside the Thai way, until unexpectedly she would erupt, and rightly so.

Songkran presented Iuu and me with an unwelcome incident when father was drunk at night, lying in the hammock, and suddenly burst out in load shouts of anger. He started screaming and cursing. The neighborhood grew quiet, people came out of their homes and surrounded father, listening to what he was screaming about but no one spoke a word.

Iuu began to weep. I sat beside her and asked her what was the matter. She didn't respond and kept on crying.

"Let's go and sleep somewhere else," I suggested, comforting her. She took no apparent notice.

The yelling got so noisy and awful that I almost decided to grab a bucket of water and pour it over Bungkert's head. Fortunately, I decided to restrain myself, simply walked up to him and asked him: "What is the matter, Bungkert?"

He looked at me in surprise as if he had just awoken from a bad dream and said to me in a quiet and collective voice: "Nothing."

A few moments later he resumed his abusive behavior until, eventually, he gave up and fell asleep.

Iuu told me months later what Bungkert's outburst was all about. He had complained about Iuu, that she was no good being married to a farang. Why was he still working, he complained, demanding of Iuu to get another farang so that she could send more money home. I was extremely embarrassed to hear that. None of the bystander ever looked at me while Bungkert was screaming. I had no idea what the nature of his anger was. Alas! we would hear more of Bungkert later.

Only once during our first year did Iuu and I have an argument that ended with her starting to pack her bag ready to leave, as was her nature: a runner. I forgot what the argument was all about. It was very emotional, though.

I felt beat and helpless, loving Iuu but not wanting to ask her that she stay. Instead, I put on shirt and trousers, ready to go side by side with her so that her leaving would lead nowhere. I was ready and sat down on the bed when my nose started to bleed. Big drops of read blood where dropping onto the floor and I made no attempts at stopping the outpouring.

Iuu saw me sitting there, head down and bleeding like a pig. She quickly got tissue and offered it to me.

"Thank you," I said. "You are a good wife." Then I put plugs into my nose to stop the blood, got up, and we embraced each other sobbing. Then I realized how much Iuu wanted to stay, wanted to be with me, didn't want to leave except to save her face. We cried a little together and said our apologies, then made love as was Iuu's custom whenever she made peace with me, which put the whole matter to rest.

All in all, the first year together with Iuu was one prolonged honeymoon. Sometimes she would say I was lucky to have her, and I replied, that so was she to have me, but in truth I knew that I was the luckier one of the two of us. We spent virtually every hour of the day together, except when I was teaching, which was not very much, or she was at school or going to see Geet while I was working on a paper, the internet, preparing for class, or grading papers. Otherwise, we were pretty much inseparable.

We took a lot of short trips to places along the ocean or the Islands of Koh Samed and my favorite island of Koh Chang, just to get away from the confinements and the work at ABAC. Sometimes we would see the parents at Klang and go to the beach at Laem Mae Pim on the Rayong Coast together, having a picnic and swimming in the ocean. We always took the bus or minibuses along the way, and I didn't seem to mind, but Iuu mentioned it several times that she wished we had a car. I was thinking about it, too. It would be nicer to escape from ABAC and we would be much more mobile. But for Iuu, I sensed, there was also the status involved that goes along with car ownership.

Iuu spoke virtually no English when we met, let alone write. After one year together she had developed a useful vocabulary for everyday use. Arguing, which was one of her strong talents, she did like a lawyer. We argued from time to time, but did not actually fight. Her standard repertoire were the following sentences in response to my questions:

"Up to you."

"Now you know."

"I don't care."

"This is Thailand."

"I didn't know myself." (A nice way of saying, "Yes, I lied to you.")

"I changed my mind." (Another term for reneging on a promise.)

"Don't think too much."

"Only talk."

"I was angry." (Meaning she didn't mean what she said.)

"I am Iuu."

"I have to care for my family."

"Husbands I can have many. But only one mother and father. (Ouch, that really hurt me.)

"When wife is happy, husband is happy."

"Only see." (Meaning vacations had no real or tangible value.)

Her repertoire would increase substantially in later years, including some very nasty terms that she would use when she was angry, or to add force to her point of view.

We celebrated our first anniversary going out for a buffet, an eat-as-much-as-you-like restaurant. She said that I was not a rich man, but we had enough, she said. She never put money in issue, except that she did not like to receive weekly allowances but rather a lump sum at the beginning of the month. I know, I micromanaged her money. Sorry, Iuu, I should have known better.

The main thing, she said, was that we were happy. And happy I think we were.

Chapter 6
Second Year at ABAC

My return ticket to Vancouver, provided by ABAC as part of the initial teaching contract, expired on April 30, 2002. The new contract provided for another return ticket as well. At the end of the trimester, "Iuu" and I flew to Vancouver, Canada, just to use up the ticket and to show her my country.

With hindsight I wouldn't make the journey again.

"Only see," was Iuu's famous response to these journeys that cost a lot of money but left no tangible value.

We could have traveled in Asia instead, including Tibet or to the Maldives or some exotic place I hadn't seen myself. I had lived in Vancouver off and on for nearly thirty years, enjoyed exciting and happy years, followed by disaster after splitting with wife number two who took our two boys away from me, so there was nothing there that I really missed, or wanted to repeat.

My second oldest son, Armin, married with two children, living in Vancouver, had been estranged when he protested against my marriage to a nineteen year-old, probably on the behest of his conservative and a few years older wife. They have a nice house in North Vancouver. The engineering firm he worked for designed the Rama XIII bridge in Bangkok, the tall free-standing cable state bridge of the kind researched by my son in his doctoral dissertation in civil engineering at Stanford University in California on the topic of active control.

"I don't want to have a sugar daddy in my family," he had emailed me.

When Iuu and I met him to pick up some of my stuff I had in storage at his house, he greeted us warmly and posed for a picture while his son, Oscar, was hiding in the living room, peaking curiously out the window. He allowed me to take a photo of him, tall slender and serious at 195 centimeters with Iuu at 162, smiling.

"Not welcome," commented Iuu on my family situation. She wasn't impressed the least. I took the emotional hit.

"I'm so happy to have you, though," I responded. She smiled back at me and said as she did so often:

"You will have me a long time."

Iuu always knew exactly how to restore my balance and make me feel happy. She was the perfect life companion and lover for me, a true friend as well. I was deeply in love with Iuu, although at times, to my present great sorrow, dismay and deep regret, in failed to remember. I failed to show her my love and affection that I had for her deep inside my heart, and that she needed and asked to be shown, while she showed me hers many times daily. Especially in year three she asked me regularly:

"Am I beautiful?"

"Yes, very beautiful," I would reply.

"Do you love me?"

I would respond with a platonic simple "yes" whereas I should have hugged and kissed her.

Armin and I had been extremely close when he was a child until he got married to Joanne at age 24. Joanne, coming from a working class family who had educated herself to become a medical typist, was a small, tough and somewhat controlling lady. I believe it was her who told Armin to disapprove of my marriage to Iuu who was nineteen at the time because it set an example she was afraid Armin might follow one day…

In contrast, my oldest son, Gunter, a Ph.D. in mechanical and aerospace engineering from Princeton, telephoned his congratulations and even spoke to Iuu on the phone after receiving the news of our marriage.

The three-hour flight to Hong Kong went by quickly. Then came the grueling haul of twelve hours to Vancouver. As the plane came in over the snow capped Coast Mountains, Iuu got very excited, took pictures of the rugged terrain below and just couldn't take her eyes off the wild nature below.

My friend Pedro Mora, who had agreed to meet us at the airport and drive us to friends were we would stay the two and a half weeks, missed us and we took the bus to town.

The whole town of over a million people seemed empty. No one was walking on the sidewalks, it seemed, and the traffic was extremely light. I asked my friends about it, whether today was a holiday or something.

"No, everything's normal. It's always like this."

I had gotten used to the hustle and bustle of Bangkok and the immensity of the compact crowds, motorcycles, cars and buses that were crammed into often narrow streets lined by vendors upon vendors selling their wares on the sidewalks. I had forgotten what a normal North American city looked like: empty!

Our friends, Nancy from Peru and Hisao from Japan – landed immigrants for decades and now Canadian citizens – gave us a room in the basement that was normally rented out to university students. We gave them a couple hundred dollars for it. The couple had two girls. Hanna, a fierce and determined little six year-old, and Sonya around twelve. They liked Iuu instantly.

The first two nights, Iuu slept in full clothes with two blankets on top. She said she was cold, and I think she was. Twenty-one degrees room temperature is normal in Canada, but for her who was used to at least twenty-five if not more, it was freezing cold. I don't think we would have any babies ever if we lived in Canada.

Iuu and I visited my friends in the Fraser Valley. She was impressed by Johanna's kitchen and baking skills and said to me she wanted to learn herself. We drove to Cypress Bowl Park on the mountains only thirty minutes away from downtown Vancouver, and skied a little in the snow. Iuu was delighted and posed for many pictures. She actually skied down a slope for about twenty meters until she landed on her bum and laughed. It was a bright and sunny day. She enjoyed it, but I don't believe for a minute that she would exchange her native Thailand for the rugged, cold, and under-populated Canada no matter how wealthy and comfortable it was.

Iuu and I took my friend of ten years, Pedro Mora, along to visit the capital city of Victoria on Victoria Island. We left my old Ford Mercury Lynx at the Tswawassen Ferry Terminal and enjoyed the two hour ferry ride across the Straight of Juan de Fuca to Swartz Bay, taking the bus to downtown Victoria.

I knew the two hundred year old city quite well, its old time charm, clean air, and had worked there as chief financial officer for a small telecommunications start-up company for a couple of months in 2000, the year before I followed ABAC's call to teach in Bangkok. For some unexplainable reason, I didn't like Victoria. It was cut off from the mainland, had an air of old age with many retired people from the West of Canada making it their place of retirement. Victoria being the seat of the provincial government had a solid income base but only light industry.

We went to Parliament Buildings. Parliament was in session. We went in and listened for about half an hour until Iuu got bored, then toured the harbor. A couple of float planes came in for landing and take off. Iuu got very excited and ran onto the dock to have a closer look.

"Flying ships," she exclaimed, grabbed my camera and took pictures.

"I have to show the pictures to my people back home," she said. "They won't believe their eyes to see flying boats."

We have a tendency in Canada and the United States to believe that the rest of the world is standing outside looking in, many people from third world countries wanting to immigrate and live in Canada. That is a misconception of reality, I believe.

Thai women who marry ferangs and move to their foreign countries, be it North America or Europe, maintain a strong relationship with their native country, and in the end all come home once they saved up enough money, either alone or with their farang husbands, starting small businesses in Thailand like hotels and restaurants. I met many such retirees in Pattaya and on Koh Samed and Koh Chang. If I was Thai, I believe I would have the same affection for my country, its easy-going life-style, food, and fun loving people. In fact, after only three years in Thailand, I think that I am unfit to return to a farang country. However distracting the traffic, noise, pollution, and population density might be, Thailand grows on you.

It's a real pity that immigration is so bureaucratic. I have to report every ninety days to the authorities that I'm still residing in Thailand, although the visa itself covers a year. Setting up a business in Thailand is a nightmare for a farang. A corporation must be fifty-one percent Thai owned although there are ways to have control by limiting voting rights on the Thai shareholders who essentially become free-loaders. It is impossible to buy real property in a farang's name or jointly with a Thai wife, although a purchase and lease-back up to thirty years would provide possession and quasi-ownership.

If Thailand only reigned in her overbearing bureaucracy and opened herself up to foreigners without discrimination, I believe Thailand would quickly become the country of choice for private investment, because of sun, sand and sea and easy going fun loving ways.

Thailand has an abundant, inexpensive, willing and easily trainable labor force, an abundance of friendly and beautiful males and females ready to engage in relationships to take them out of poverty or advance their lifestyles, has superb beaches in the south, charming mountains in the north, inexpensive food and accommodation, and is in general the imperfectly perfect, or perfectly imperfect, last paradise left on this hectic planet.

I am lucky that I am in demand as an educator with skills in international accounting and finance because I speak the global language which is English.

I am lucky that I am a foreign-educated farang. And I am especially lucky to have a young and beautiful, open-minded and energizing wife, my Love Iuu. But under the pressures of the daily routine, driven by my German trained ambition for improvement and success, I often and easily forget that I already have everything a man in my stage of life could ever want or hope for and simply relax, saying "Sabai sabai…," "take it easy, what comes, comes…"

To my deep regret and dismay, I have yet to learn living the pleasure and fun seeking, easy going, Thai life style, and since I haven't done so yet, often I am not understood by my wife and her family, and become the recipient of great suffering.

"There is no mercy in Asia," a colleague and former diplomat told me. Thai people bury their emotions and keep them hidden deep inside to keep face and not expose themselves to risk until, one day, they erupt and it's game over. But more about that part later.

Chapter 7
Caring for Mother

We returned from Vancouver to Bangkok in early May 2002. I remember the feeling of joy and happiness in both Iuu and myself when the plane came in for a landing at Bangkok, the lush and illuminated countryside and city below us, and when we touched down and stepped on Thai soil again, it felt like a true home-coming to the country we both loved and needed. And above all, we loved, appreciated and needed each other, Iuu and I.

Iuu's way to reach her goals in life were to marry a farang. All the women of Nonglard who had done so had a house, money, and were doing well but not living at home or in Thailand as we did, but abroad with their husband; mostly the United States, England, Germany or Scandinavia.

Older farang, she said was okay. I knew she preferred somewhat older men. I saw the Marlboro man's picture on the wall of her bedroom, but there were also posters of young male Thai movie stars, and two children hugging each other.

Iuu's first goal and purpose in life was to care for her mother and father. Father was incidental, but mother came first. This determination is so deep and unshakable in her soul, that I wonder how it got there in the first place because in Europe or North America, children don't care for their parents except in special situations, but parents give to their children so they can marry and have a home for the grandkids. White farang parents are normally well cared for through state pensions and company retirement schemes.

Mother must have implanted the idea in Iuu's mind when Iuu was very young, repeating and repeating it, and having it reinforced by the practice in other families. Therefore, it was alright when mother and father retired early to Nonglard at an age much younger than my own. That was her parent's choice and none of our business whose duty it was to provide.

Iuu's second goal was to provide a new house for her mother. Father's don't own anything, except may be a motorcycle. That's all.

It was my wish to build a house on our mango farm first, something for ourselves because mother and father already had home, although it was getting old having been constructed only fifteen years ago. Iuu's immediate question was:

"Can mother and father live in it?"

I made a very grave mistake by replying: "I don't have good experiences with mother-in-laws living in the same house, and in my country we discourage that. So no, I think it's a bad idea."

I explained how my first wife's mother was the disrupting force behind our eventual divorce, did not like me from the start, and meddled in our marriage by influencing her daughter and having a say in her feelings, decisions, and just about everything. No, no, I said, not again please.

Iuu was shocked I learned later, but said nothing. The subject came up again and again. Iuu tried to explain to me that as the oldest daughter it was her duty to care for mother. There is no state pension or retirement fund in Thailand or Asia in general, I believe. The children are the old age insurance. Because the boys leave the parental home to live with their wife and help her to provide for her parents, the whole burden falls on the oldest daughter, the younger daughters assisting with money.

One of Iuu's favorite past times at our home was to draw floor plans of our future home on the mango farm. I went through all her notebooks from school, and there were pages upon pages in every other book in which variations of the same floor plans are drawn.

The house loomed very large in her mind, almost like an obsession. I now believe that I made a big mistake in not addressing the issue enough, putting away money in our joint account on a regular basis as we had done a year earlier for the purchase of the two-*rai* (one acre) mango farm in Nonglard.

I had even insisted that Iuu give me a thirty-year lease-back on the land because I had read many stories on the internet and in books that Isan women typically marry farang for money, stay with him until the money runs out, and then find a new one. As a precaution, before I had the soil put on the land to build the house on during Songkran in April 2003, I insisted and after much wrangling invoking the mayor's assistance, obtain the lease that we then registered at the land titles' office of the Amphur in Nonghan. The official took Iuu aside and asked why she did this, as it was never done before. As a result, Iuu was not only humiliated but must have also felt ridiculed.

With hindsight, my precautions were justified but may have also contributed and sparked the situation I found myself in later where Iuu started to begin to reject me. My precautions came from reading and from my own thoughts. Iuu had not given me any reason to believe that she would ever leave me for another man, or not toughen it out if we ran out of money, or because the going got rough.

Iuu's father, Bungkert, was a witness to the wrangling and witnessed our signatures on the lease, but said nothing, which is typical of the Thai way.

Much later he told me, though: "Michael, any other woman would have long left you, except Iuu."

Instead of being mindful, I thought that Iuu had a concern of me leaving her because she was envied by many another Isan woman not only in her village. But the truth and reality was quite the opposite and the other way around. I did not know, perhaps I was stupid, not wanting to know, either. It takes time to learn the Thai, in particular the Isan, ways, and I was a slow learner.

Watch your thoughts because they may become words. Watch your words because they may become actions.

Iuu's goal number three, I believe, was to make me, her husband, happy, but the goal was circular in a way because she said many times:

"When the wife is happy, the husband is happy."

The purpose of goal number three, making me happy, was to help Iuu with her goals one and two, namely to care for mother, and incidentally father, although her father, Bungkert, became a burdensome problem because of his loose and careless attitude towards the family and behavior, as we will see, and she never really liked him having grown up without him during her earlier childhood.

Iuu's affirmations of her love for me that even increased in intensity over the years, I was so stupid as no to recognize and affirm, but also to put into question in answer to her questions: "Do you love me?"

Not knowing how to respond, I explained love for another as helping the other through his or her life, while in truth she loved me from the heart. I have no excuse for my misguided thinking. Being a certified public accountant, perhaps, carries the professional hazard of doubt, doubt until removed by proof. Perhaps this doubt of her love was a protection against my own deep love of her which, I was afraid, might not be returned because her love for me might only be an end to the means of caring for mother and gathering up money and wealth through land, house, and whatever.

As the Prah had told me, "If you love a woman, you have to be smart," the first thing on the agenda of a long love life is to meet the basic needs of the loved one, and help her in meeting what is required of her, and in Isan that is caring for mother. Once that need has been met, I believe, the love of the woman if the man can be loved is all for her husband.

Iuu's goal number four was earning the respect of her villagers by prestigious means of possessions, education and the status it conveys.

Iuu's goal number five was finally what for the European, and even more so the American or Canadian woman, would be goal number one, namely self-actionalization, to lead her life her way and for herself, not for others.

I have read and believe myself that Isan women including Iuu were brought up for self-sacrifice so that the rural family, traditionally mired in poverty had the prospect of survival. Men being excluded from that duty except as the helper's helper for their wives, therefore rank third behind their mother-in-law and wife, and they know it.

An Isan husband never sees his salary, which is paid to the wife or her bank account. She would return to him an allowance for *laokhao*, smokes, would select and buy his clothes and shoes and give him money for things he asked for and she approved of.

When Bungkert was desirous of fun away from home, he would steal the money by packing rice in bags, sell it to the mill and not come home until the money was gone. Or he would open the gas from the stove, hold a lighter in his hand and threaten Tang with exploding the house unless she gave him the money, or he would simply box her.

Isan is a matriarchal society. Europe and North America are emerging from a patriarchal one where the roles are reversed.

Some time after our return from Canada, Iuu and I suffered a serious incident that nearly broke our young marriage. It was also sparked by Isan tradition of helping the extended family in any and every way she could.

I had made the mistake of inviting a plump and bold middle-aged American prof into our home. Iuu had cooked for us and we talked over a couple of beers, Iuu listening in attentively by now understanding every word of the English that was spoken.

Stephen was a loaner and said he was interested in meeting a Thai lady. We kept on talking and laughing when I noticed Iuu was on the phone in the background talking in Isan. By now I could distinguish between Thai and Isan, the local dialect of the North East that is also spoken and understood in Laos.

I heard Iuu was talking to her girl cousin Kai from Nonglard next door, the daughter of her mother's brother, Lod, and his wife Thien who was a notorious gambler and had lost the money Kai's husband had been sending home from Taiwan so the two could build a house for themselves when he cam home. Kai had a six-year-old son, Wai, whom she raised herself at home, something that would normally be her mother's duty so that she could receive more money being sent home to her.

The typical work of a daughter with only a grade six education would be on their farm planting and harvesting rice or cutting sugar, both infrequent and paid low, working in a factory in Bangkok such as a fish processing or shrimp packing plant, on construction in the city mixing sand and concrete or carrying material around the site, or, the last and best paying job, namely working as a bar girl, say "prostitute", in Pattaya or Phuket, sometimes Bangkok.

Mother Thein, who was a smoothie and always came up to me when I was in Nonglard touching me softly on the arm and talking sweetly, had been urging and even beating Kai to go to Pattaya and find a farang just like Iuu had.

Kai's brother Olee had also been working in Taiwan, come home at New Year's and bought himself a second-hand pickup truck that he ditched during the same holidays in his drunken stupor. Then mother had borrowed a hundred thousand baht at five percent interest a month giving the family home as security. The money was used to pay an employment agency that sent Olee to Israel to work and send money home. But Olee returned in a few weeks, saying there was no work. The scheme had been a scam by the employment agency to wring money out the poor who could least afford it: always the people of Isan.

Eventually, in about August 2002, soft spoken and timid Kai, about 24 years old, who was chubby if not even fat, began to listen to her mother's demand and tried to fly to Germany at first to find work but was refused the visa.

Then, in November 2002, came Iuu's call.

"There's an American farang here at ABAC who wants to meet you. Get on the bus immediately and come to see me. I'll introduce you to him."

The following day Iuu told me that Kai was coming for a visit. I understood immediately what that meant and demanded of Iuu to call Kai who was already on the bus to return home and forget about visiting us. My argument was that as a professor I could not tolerate Kai at he university, fucking herself into money. That the only reason Iuu and I could live here together was that we were married, and so on, and on.

Two things were against me. First, my misguided morality in which I didn't even believe myself. Second, fear.

I was ignoring the Buddhist teachings I had received five years back in Vancouver from the Venerable Sister Ann McNeil:

We always get what we really, really wish and hope for. But also get what we fear the most."

In our case, my fear of the events was actually the inducer of bringing them about. Fear is the worst motivator for anything, and my fear was that by helping Kai to get into money by screwing around, Iuu herself might get a bad idea, after all hadn't we first met in Pattaya?

"Kai is already on the bus and now in Nakhon Ratchasima. She will be hear in a few hours," lamented Iuu.

"Call her on the mobile and tell her to return home."

"No," was Iuu's blunt reply.

"Why not? Kai is married, has a child, and her husband is working in Taiwan sending money home," I reasoned.

"He's not sending money home anymore. If I don't welcome Kai and help her, the family does not like me anymore. I must help my family," reasoned Iuu.

"But hadn't you called in the first place, the problem would not have arisen. Why did you call?" I thundered.

"Now it happened," was Iuu's simple and direct answer.

Iuu was right. I gave up on condition that Iuu would not introduce Kai to the American farang, Stephen, but let her figure out for herself why she had come. I wasn't logical in my reasoning because obviously Kai could not have spent the time and money to come to Bangkok and return empty-handed. At that time I was not aware that her mother, Thein, was pushing Kai.

We experienced one of our unexpected and undeserved setbacks. For Iuu it was progress with an unexpected delay. I don't remember we made love that night. It was sacrificed on the altar of helping her cousin to care for her mother, the age-old Isan orientation that I began to understand but refused to accept or support on grounds of a false morality.

With hindsight I should have been frank with Iuu. I should have given her to understand that I did not like her helping anyone in the fucking business because I didn't want her to even think of returning to it. The following month we talked about what had happened and she agreed not to help Kai anymore, saying:

"Now I am Madam. Pattaya is behind me. Finished."

Kai arrived. Iuu enjoyed her company, cooking Isan food, talking on end, and eventually watching the Thai soap movie on ITV Channel 3 together. Kai was put up in Tiu's room I had rented for her brother a few blocks away, returning in the morning and stay all day.

This went on for a couple of days, almost a week. One day when I was teaching I received a call from Iuu that she and Kai were on their way to visit Kai's brother Olee in a suburb of Bangkok, and that Iuu would not be coming home at night.

I made an almost fatal mistake by ordering Iuu to return immediately, or, when she refused to ask her the address and telephone number of Olee so that I could pick her up at night and bring her home in our new Ford Ranger pickup that we had bought in August.

Iuu replied that Kai was looking for the address and phone number and would call me back.

Eventually, during a second conversation Iuu said they didn't have the address but gave me the phone number.

I called Olee in the evening and couldn't really converse because he spoke almost no English. But neither Iuu or Kai were at his house. He kept mentioning "Aya", "Aya" but I had not idea where that was. Iuu's mobile was shut off.

It was an awful feeling to spend the night alone not knowing where Iuu was. Iuu punished me by keeping her phone turned off so that I could not reach her. I thought about a means of punishing her back, even shocking her, and after class on Sunday morning, bagged all of her belongings into cardboard boxes and plastic bags, and drove them to Nonglard arriving early in the morning.

When Kai's mother Thein saw me arriving without Iuu, she went white. At that time I had no idea that Thein was the driving force behind sending Kai, who was married and had a son, to work in the sex trade. A villager who spoke a little English came up to me and I told him the story that Iuu had left with Kai to go fucking in Pattaya and that I was bringing all of Iuu's belongings home. Then I went into Iuu's room, which by now was also mine, and slept for a couple of hours, then drove all the way back to Bangkok, arriving at midnight. Iuu's mother and father where living in Klang near Rayong. They were not in Nonglard.

I learned later that my move had shocked Iuu who didn't expect my reaction. She did not answer my calls, but her family's calls from Nonglard went through and they told her. Then she called me and asked if she could have a one-week vacation alone.

"Iuu," I said, fearing for the worst by allowing a bad example, "I don't like you going on vacation alone, you know that.

But I will always care for you, always. I will put some money on your ATM card so that you are not broke."

I was actually out of myself, picked up Tiu and drove to Klang to their parents, inviting them to join us on a two day vacation on Koh Samed hoping that if Iuu heard of it, she would join us. The parents refused because tomorrow was pay day. In actual fact, they had never been on any vacation, let alone stay in nice hotels, and would have been very uncomfortable.

Tiu and I went alone. We caught the last boat to Koh Samed, and on impulse I, who didn't have a mobile at the time, called Iuu from a public pay phone, and by putting it to her learned where she was:

"You are in Pattaya, are you not?" I asked her outright.

"Yes," she replied.

"I will pay you 5,000 baht if you come and join Tiu and me tomorrow morning."

"No."

"Why not"?

"I'm here with Kai." Then she hung up.

That lonely losing feeling started rising from my belly that I experience when the person I love the most, desperately miss, and am afraid of losing, cannot be reached. But at least I knew where she was, and took a speedboat back to Ban Phe on the mainland, then drove the Ford Ranger at high speeds over the freeway and was in Pattaya about an hour after the call from Koh Samed. Then I called Iuu again.

"I'm in Pattaya, too, and want to see you."

"No. I don't want to see you." She had me lock, stock and barrel. We talked some more. She hung up. I called again. We talked some more. She hung up. This went on for about an hour with intervals of silence in between. Then Tiu and I began searching for her starting with the beer bars near the Sureena Hotel in Soi Post Office where we had taken a room, the hotel Iuu and I used to frequent when we took a break from ABAC and spent a few days on the beach in Pattaya.

We couldn't find her and her phone was turned off. She later admitted that we passed each other on Walking Street but that she quickly turned her head to the side so I wouldn't recognize her. I thought that was awful, even when she told me later.

Somehow, I reached her again and she wrung the following concessions out of me.

"How much are you paying mother and father each month," she demanded.

"The same five thousand baht. I think is okay." I said.

"When are we building our house?" she inquired.

"Next year, Iuu. First the soil has to settle."

"But mother's house is in bad shape and I want mother to have a new home," she argued.

"Then we will make two homes, Iuu. One for mother first, and then one for us."

"Okay, I will see you at the Sureena tomorrow evening," Iuu responded.

"Iuu, I'm in Pattaya. What are you doing all day? I love you. We are married. I miss you," I lamented.

"Okay, I see you at noon."

I was afraid she might be partying all night and whatever else, and that losing feeling rose up from my stomach again.

"I want you to come at nine in the morning, please."

Eventually she agreed, but it was almost noon before she surfaced.

When she did, it was heavenly. She did not return my hugs and kisses with any intensity, but there she was and I was happy, talking of our future plans and trying to make her happy, too.

She was lying on the bed and soon fell asleep. I looked at her and could not take my eyes off my wife.

'So beautiful, so young, so gorgeous are you,' I thought. 'I almost lost you, my Love. I will always love you, and will never be careless again. I promise.'

After lunch, later in the afternoon we returned home to ABAC. It was the sweetest homecoming we've had. I was forewarned what she was capable of. I watched myself to make sure I was nice and obliging. Our love for each other came back, and a little later I was becoming the old fool that I was again, and she was without power.

Yes, she had acted secretly in leaving with Kai, but said she intended to stay in Pattaya only one night to show her where to go, to introduce her, and then come home the following morning. She said if she had told me first I would have disapproved and Kai would not know what to do, and would have had to return to Nonglard empty-handed. I believe that's exactly what she intended, but my strong demands of her immediate return left her no choice but to ignore me. Nonglard had called her that I had returned all off her belongings which shocked her, but she could do nothing about it, only felt humiliated.

Iuu is an honest person who never set me up, except to make demands that were justified like building the house for mother. Iuu means well and sees both her family's and my needs. She always tried to make me happy when she could, only argue sometimes and even scream when she couldn't hold her problems inside herself anymore. Many women, including Western women, plan, scheme and lie. Iuu never did, nor do I believe she ever will. Whatever unfortunate incidents we both suffered were always the instant result of some stupid event, remark of mine, argument over nothing much in substance, and then she reacted. I was her senior by decades, but I was also insensitive to her needs, and unmindful how lucky I really was to have her.

Then she yelled at me:

"Look at you, ugly old man, how stupid you are."

Or: "Stay alone."

Or: "No one can live with you."

I hurt to hear it from her and she said: "I want to hurt you."

Because she wanted to hurt I believed that what she said was untrue. But it wasn't. I was stupid to over-react and over-state my case when in truth I was so deeply in love with her, and wanted her so much to be my wife and live together only with Iuu for a very long time. My question whether she loved me from the heart, my fear that she might return to work the nightlife in Pattaya, were making me weak and were influencing my thoughts and behavior. Iuu is so well liked by everyone who meets her, I noticed many, many times, it can only be because people feel energized by her presence, her honest smile and beautiful manner. Only I, in times of small trouble, failed to show the grace to accept her. But no anger ever stayed longer than a minute or more, because I deeply loved her. And she said the same to me, many times, many times.

Iuu and I went shopping for evening dresses for her from time to time, we were attending the ABAC seminars in Pattaya or Hua Hin together, went to faculty dinners and receptions. The faculty got used to the fact that Iuu always accompanied me, and they liked her. She made friends with a few lady professors at the graduate school of business who always came to her when we arrived and inquired how things were going.

One evening at a dinner party by a lake, President Brother Bancha came to our table. Iuu was sitting a few chairs away from me, and after chatting with us Brother Bancha asked Iuu in English:

"And what are you teaching?

The faculty burst out in laughter and replied:

"She is teaching Dr. Michael. She is his wife."

Iuu met all of the top brass of ABAC in the elevator of our building also known as "ABAC Hotel". They chatted briefly with her. All of the cleaning staff at ABAC and the guards, mostly from Isan, knew, greeted and talked to her. She drove our car anywhere in Bangkok, and was generally accepted as an important person.

In spite of this, she sometimes lamented:

"I am Madam, but I have nothing."

What she meant was a house, a bank account with enough money in it that she could buy things on the spur of the moment, a car of her own.

I told her she had more than any other young woman from Nonglard that I knew. She didn't respond. Thinking about it, she was right. The proper thing for me to do was to keep a certain amount of money in a joint bank account that either she or I could take out and spend, rather than giving her an allowance. Thai law does not permit joint land ownership, but I cured that through a leaseback of the mango farm while title to the land remained in her name. Upon my death she would have the whole thing for herself, but that's only a prospect.

If she had a wish, she said, it was that I believe her. She sensed that I was a control person and she was right. I know now she never thought of other men. Her older lady friend Geet confirmed it. It was I who made up these concerns and fears that inflicted pain on me for no reason. Iuu was believable and I should have believed her or it would hurt both her and me. I was the problem, not she.

We went to Nonglard for New Years 2002 and stayed a good week. We bought small presents for each other. But the greatest present in which Iuu truly rejoiced was a big teddy bear that I gave her in a big box wrapped in gift paper. She had no idea what was inside. When she opened it she laughed and said in a loud happy voice:

"Oh, a teddy bear. Exactly what I always wanted and never got!"

She kissed and hugged me as if I had bought her a Mercedes-Benz.

This is Iuu on the outside: Big in stature for Thai measures with strong arms and legs with thighs that are gorgeous and sexy, very tender wrists and ankles, determined but with an engaging open smile, and loud voice only if she needs one.

And this is Iuu on the inside: Smart with a good grasp of reality, honest, devoted, loving and tender, and therefore easily hurt. She keeps unpleasant things buried in her soul, and can anger quickly, but then forgets. She says she does not forgive, but my heart tells me that she tries.

Iuu said if she would ever marry again it only be for money. In other words, it was too painful to marry from the heart.

Oh, Iuu, I am sorry, so sorry, if I am the reason for your disappointment because I love you as I have never loved before.

I love you, Iuu, your fresh and engaging appearance, your beautiful looks, and above all your heart.

I love it when you say: "You have me for a long time."

I am aware of my shortcomings, now, through the unbearable hurt and pain of your absence.

I have learned my lesson well and will be your caring and loving husband until life fades. And when we are reborn, as we who are Buddhists both believe, I will marry you again and have many children who will be exactly like you so that there will be more to care for and love.

When we married in June of 2001, "Iuu", just nineteen and a half years old, was a pretty and alert teenager like one fresh out of high school. In our third year, she was growing into a beautiful young woman.

She said many times that at first, when a couple marries, there may be no love or love may be small, but then love comes by living together. I did not understand what exactly she meant because for my part I loved her from the moment I saw her.

I now know that Iuu was referring to herself. She married her first older Isan husband out of a call of duty. Her father was serving a two-year prison sentence for having caused the death of five people in Kaoh Yai National Park driving a truck in which he could have died when the truck went into a ravine. He escaped and fled the scene of the accident. She simply said she married "Bog" (I don't remember the exact name) because it was the right thing to do.

At one time she mentioned to me that she had married me for my money, being a farang. She also said that she had prayed to her Prah as a teenager to please give her a farang in marriage. She was well prepared when I proposed to her and accepted almost instantly. Sometimes during our first year, she said she loved me. In year three, her love and affection were more obvious. She came to kiss me many times during the day, and would always embrace me in bed. Then she would say:

"I love you so very, very much," and squeeze me. I would reply by saying to Iuu:

"I love you, too," and I did, very deeply so, although I did not always show it.

When we had sex she took some time to open, then eventually gather momentum and, I felt, a deep sensation, finishing by reaching her climax usually before me. In our third year we knew each other so intimately well that love-making was easy and always fulfilling.

She mentioned to her older lady friend, Geet, who later told me that sometimes Iuu considered herself reduced by me to a servant for sexual gratification, and I am puzzled to this day what exactly she meant because I never felt she was anything but my adorable soul mate and partner in love from the heart as well as the body, the two being inseparable for me.

I have never made love to a woman in my life who I wasn't in love with. We may both have felt arousals and made love without foreplay and kissing. Yes, it happened. But often, very often she became so aroused, as did I, that she said: "I can fuck you all night."

No, Iuu, you have never been only a sex object of lust for me, but always my soul mate and sex followed as a result of my deep feelings, attachment and sense of belonging to you.

Yes, sometimes, I came home from work tired, and all you had to do to get me going was put on a sex movie that we both watched in anticipation of the joy we would experience ourselves moments later. In the old days a couple would listen to romantic music, light candles and have a glass of wine together to put themselves into the mood for love. The movies were a rather direct approach leading to the same end, but completely innocent.

If you think the big black cock of the size of a pony's doing it with a couple of sexy young blondes would turn me on? May be when we first watched it, but for my part, soon after, after we had made love, it was actually a turnoff, and I physically turned off the movie because it could not contribute anything to what we had shared and given each other.

No, the sex object might have been the fantasy in your own mind referring to the movie, but it was never you in my mind but quite to the contrary.

One notoriously shrewd and successful sex worker is Iuu's friend, Chompoo from the neighboring village of Nongmek.

Iuu says there is no man in Nongmek left who Chompoo, meaning "pink" in Thai, hadn't slept with. She has a pretty daughter age seven or eight from one of them, showing that Chompoo, is a year younger than Iuu, began her "career" at the tender age of around fourteen. The baby is raised by Chompoo's mother in Nongmek where Chompoo returns regularly throughout her working year. She does not have houses built for her like most Isan working women do, locally known as "puyin hakin" ("galllie" is the word for "whore" and seldom heard as a rather rude term), instead, said Iuu, she spends whatever is left over after paying mother on her Thai boyfriends.

I am not sure why because I was told and believed that Isan women prefer farang. At least that was Iuu's statement all along. In reality, however, it appears as confirmed by one of my Thai male friends, as in any other country, given a choice, local women prefer local men. On the other hand Isan men are notoriously known for drinking, fighting when drunk, and laziness. They are said to take mistresses whenever they can afford, while the farang is true to his Thai wife, cares for the family, is industrious, and does not fight. But above all, the farang has money, exactly the kind of aphrodisiac Isan lusts for.

I met Champoo the first time when Iuu and I visited Nonglard at Songkran, in April 2002. We squatted down on a rice mat beside the street, and she asked me in fairly good English, looking at me with an innocent face and a faint and curious smile:

"How can I meet farang?" as if she didn't already know. I had no idea at the time and was thinking that Champoo desired to follow in Iuu's successful footsteps.

"There are many internet sites that will post your picture and email address, and then you simply wait," I replied.

The next time Iuu and I were in Nonglard, a few months later, Champoo arrived in the company of a thirty year-old Dutch man by the name of Rick. His father had a factory in Holland and he was obviously well of and looked like a good prospective husband for Chompoo who seemed to be, or behaved, like being in love with him. Rick made no bones about loving and adoring Chompoo.

I listened to Rick's story. He came to Thailand to visit his mother who, in her fifties, lived in Pattaya and was divorced from his father. There he met Chompoo in a disco claiming that she was visiting a girl friend. He fell in love with her instantly, and she had the kindness, he said, to stay over in Pattaya just for him until his return flight a week later. Of course, he gave her money because she came from the poorhouse of Thailand, Isan. And he sent money regularly after their first meeting, so that she could live a little more

Iuu, June 6, 2001, after arriving in Nonglard. Right: With mother Tang-on

Villagers in Nonglard welcoming me. Iuu not home.

Michael and Iuu
June 7, 2001 in
Nonglard

Mother Tang-on
Father Bungkert
Iuu and Michael

At the Great Wat
in Bangkok

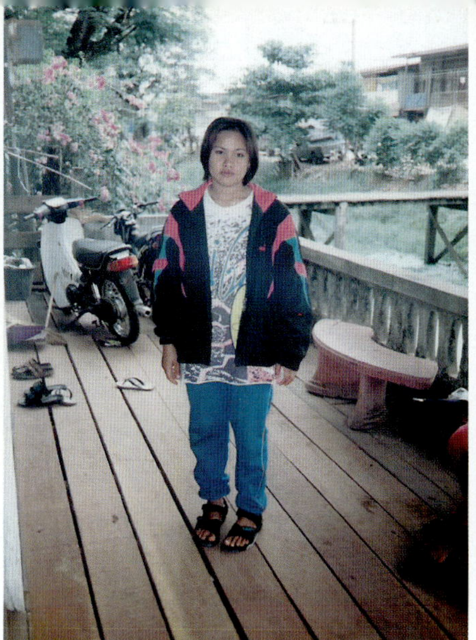

Iuu at 17 in Nonghan, Undon Thani

Wedding Photo June 2001. Iuu 19

At Assumption University in Bangkok, Hua Mark

At home in our studio at ABAC, 2001

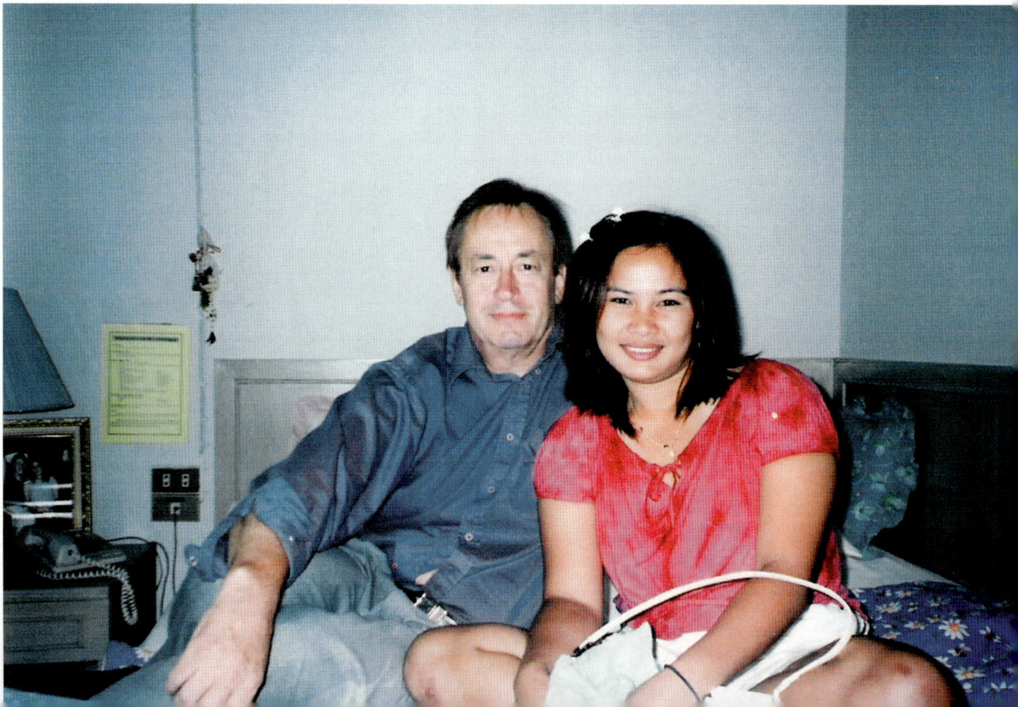

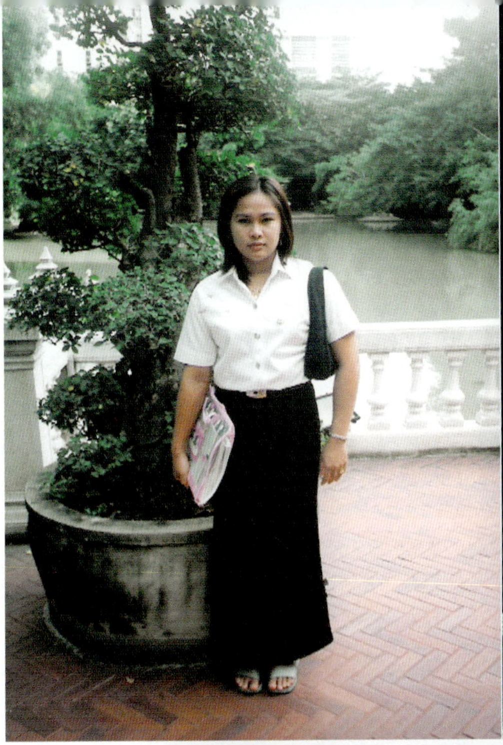

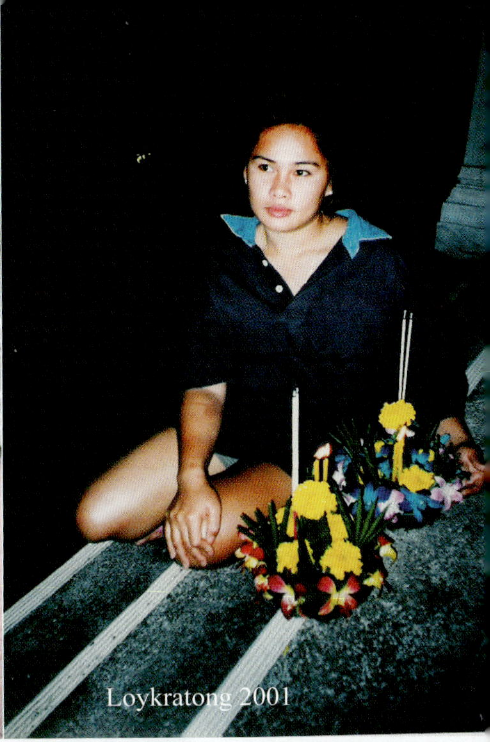

Iuu's 20th birthday
September 2001

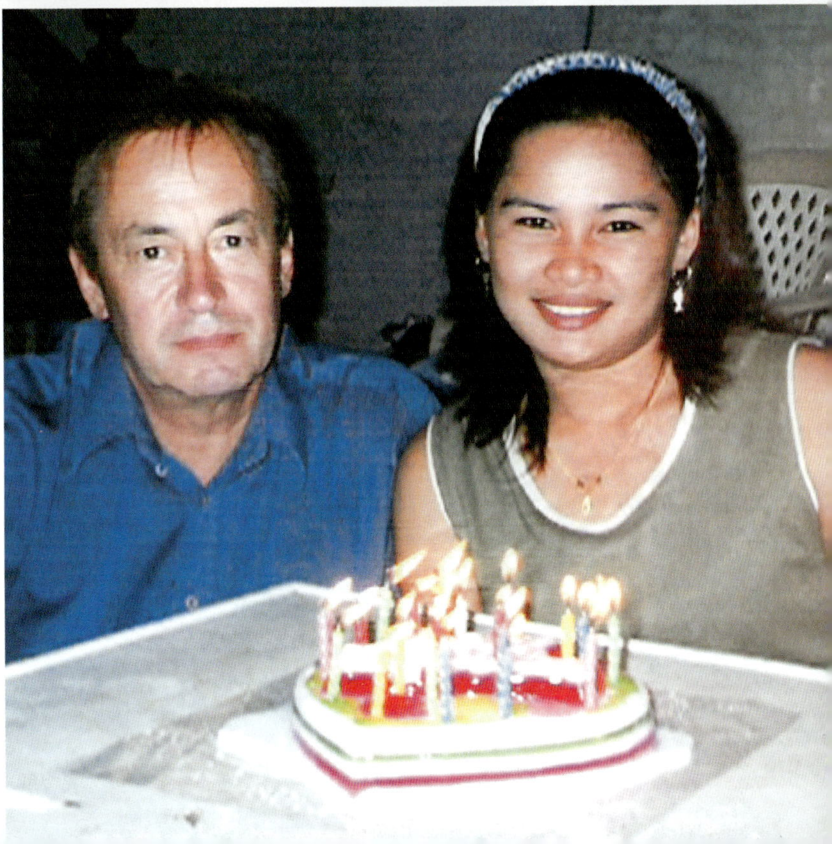

Michael and Iuu
November, 2001
at a dinner party

Michael posing with
ABAC's Thai dancing
class

Iuu at ABAC's
swimming pool, 2001
She did learn to swim
very well.

Cover Picture
At Sattahip, February 2004
At the MBA freshman seminar, Dusit Beach Resort in Pattaya February 2002

During Songkran
in Nonglard
April 2002

Rice Planting
in Nonglard
June 2002

Iuu at Rice
Harvest in
Nonglard
November 2002

On Koh Samed 2001

On koh Chang, February 2002

Iuu cooking on the floor

Iuu's favorite past time: eating

Our two-rai (one acre) mango farm in Nonglard April 2002

In Iuu's name. Michael's 30-year registered lease

Putting soil on for our house: 105 truck loads in April 2003

April 2003
in Nonglard

Iuu, 21, with her friend, Champoo, 20

With Dao and her borhter,'s a school teacher, and Iuu in Sakonakorn, January 2003

Left. On Grouse Mountain
Vancouver, B.C., Canada,
Howe Sound, Horsehoe Bay
near Vancouver, and in
Victoria, B.C., Canada

Right: At Cypress Bowl Park,
Vancouver, Canada
Iuu's first time in the snow
and on skiis

Below: In Victoria, B.C.

May 2002

Iuu getting her driver's license in December 2002

Iuu "in the center", her brother Tiu, Mother Tang-on & Father Bungkert Klaeng, December 2002

Iuu and Michael in Germany
June-July 2003

Iuu with her dream car: a Mercedes Benz
Gensungen, Kassel, Germany June 2003

Jungfrau Mountain from Kleine
Scheidegg, Grindelwald, Switzerland

Wat Phra That Doi Suthep,
Chiang Mai, December 30, 2003
Iuu with aunt in Nonglard, January 2004
Mountain tribe people, Northern Thailand
Iuu's new 3 million baht
house on soi Nern Plubwan
in Pattaya, end of May 2004

comfortable and not look for another man. I think Rick considered himself engaged to Chompoo or something like that, meaning he had expressed his intention to marry her, and she must have smiled back at him in sweet anticipation, and then some.

Rick, Chompoo, Iuu and I went to a karaoke outside Nongmek together, sang, drank and had fun. After three hours, Chompoo was drunk. I was asked to drive Iuu and myself home in her pickup truck, that she drove without a driver's license perfectly well, as Rick was inexperienced and scared of driving on the left side of the road as is the rule in Thailand. Chompoo slept all the way.

Iuu and Chompoo were good friends. Iuu said Chompoo was not greedy, but enjoyed Thai men and liked to spend all the money she had rather than saving it up for a house, land, and cars like most of the Isan *puyin hakin* or "working girls". Iuu considered her "honest", I do not, at least not in matters of the heart and the other parts. I told Iuu that I didn't want to meet Chompoo anymore. Iuu got my point, said she would obey my wishes, but I knew too well that Iuu maintained her own opinion which was, "Chompoo is a good friend of mine. Her way of life is none of our business."

Thinking to myself, I agreed with Iuu, but was motivated by my old fear that Chompoo's words might influence Iuu's thinking, and that the words could lead to actions, namely, Iuu's return to Pattaya herself at one point in time. I was not too wrong in my assessment, but it was not Chompoo who influenced Iuu, but my own shortcomings in my daily life with Iuu, small as they may have appeared to me at the time.

Every time Iuu and I were in Nonglard, it only took a day or two for Chompoo to appear if she was home, too. I believe it was Songkran again, the year 2003, when Iuu broke the news that Chompoo had changed from her old loose ways because she had just married a man from America. I agreed, that, indeed, would be a change and we decided to visit the couple in Champoo's home in Nongmek.

Chompoo welcomed us and the first words she spoke to me were, "I miss Rick, I love Rick, I wished he was here…"

I believed it was a show as much as Chompoo was speaking the truth. I think Rick, had he wanted Chompoo for his wife, should have understood the Isan soul and married her, not waited. He had come one more time to be with Chompoo who had picked him up at the airport as her long lost lover, but he couldn't make up his mind. His father, he said, was going to disown him if he moved to Thailand, because he was needed in the business, and Chompoo did not want to live in Holland. She was right. I'm sure she loved her country, had a couple of boyfriends who sent her money every month believing she would stay home waiting for them to return. It was more exciting and easier to simply stay in Thailand, keep the sex mill going, and rake in the money from more and more sources. If two of her lovers arrived at the same time, there would be time enough to make a choice among those she wanted to keep, and those to let go.

Iuu was somewhat disappointed because the man, a steel worker from Iowa or some mid-Western town, divorced and in his mid-thirties was not a bit handsome but, she said, ugly. He sat somewhat forlorn all by himself away from Chompoo's family and I sensed things weren't the way he had expected. There was no kissing and hugging between him and Chompoo as one would expect of newly-weds.

He had been corresponding with Chompoo by email and decided to come to Thailand two weeks ago to see her in person, fell in love with her, and married her at the Amphur on the spot. There was a slight problem, though. The American embassy refused Chompoo a visitor's visa by reason that she was now married and would not return to Thailand, overstaying her visitor's status in America. The poor man had made the wrong application, I told him. Had you not married in Thailand first, but asked for a fiancée's visa to marry Chompoo in the United States, the visa would have been granted, no problem.

I asked him how he appeared in front of immigrations, with shirt and tie, together with a lawyer, or in blue jeans with an open shirt and sandals?

"I'm on vacation, man. I went in jeans and runners. The Thai assistants were rude to me," he complained, "and I am an American. This is my Embassy, not theirs."

"Go again," I suggested. "Take an American lawyer with you. Might cost you a few hundred bucks, and wear a tie and shirt, proper shoes, and may be even a jacket. That always impresses the Thai mentality."

"Okay, will do," he replied. "I don't get it. Now we are married, that should give us status and a higher ranking than being only engaged."

"I don't get it either, except that visitors' visas are just that, for visit and return. But Chompoo had been in the States before to visit her sister and returned. They should have granted the visa, but then again, they are right. Now that she's married to you why would she want to return to Thailand. Isn't it natural for a woman to want to live with her husband?"

He agreed. It was a SNAFU (a "Situation Normal All Fucked Up").

We visited the newly weds again on the following day, and Scott as his name was, complained that Chompoo was uncooperative in filling out the immigration forms just in case the visitor's visa was not granted. He said she was even rude to him. Then he asked me about Thai women and whether I thought Chompoo would be faithful if he had to go home alone.

I replied in the traditional Thai fashion if you don't want to say anything negative or lie: "I don't know."

"I guess they're the same as in the States. There is not one woman who doesn't cheat on her husband, given the opportunity," Scott said with a resigned voice.

I nodded in sympathy and understanding.

Scott went home alone and Chompoo didn't appear to mind in the least, I heard. In fact she was at it again in Pattaya and came to visit us at ABAC following her application for a visitor's visa to Germany to see a new boyfriend by the name of Raimund. She came to our room at ABAC and we decided to take her with us on our short vacation to Koh Samed together with another visiting lady professor from Poland who was nice company, always, Dr. Sophia.

The Koh Samed vacation went alright, except that Chompoo got completely drunk at the disco and Iuu, being somewhat of a follower of hers, tried to imitate her but I held her back as good I could. After we retired to our room, Chompoo went on a man hunt. Whether she found anyone or not, I don't know, but Sophia observed that she came home very late at night, or rather early in the morning, completely blitzed and making a lot of noise until she found the bed in the room they were sharing.

In the spring of 2004, Chompoo finally got her visa and visited her legal husband, Scott, in America. She stayed for a month or two and went back to Thailand to practice her old profession. Scott calls her every day in Nongmek on the land line, making sure she's home. Whatever excuses she offers him when she's not at home is anybody's guess. She told him of her visit to Germany, but did not mention Raimund, Iuu said, rather it was on a sort of "my friend is sick" basis.

When I am told someone is "sick" in Thailand, to send money for the doctor and the medicine, I've learned to be careful. Isan people don't spread the bad news but keep it to themselves. They only call when they are fine. It has to do with image, I guess. They don't want to be known or seen as having a problem.

I had promised Iuu that I would show her Europe one day. The occasion arose in June 2003 when I thought I better pick up the oil paintings that I had left in storage in Germany with one of my older brothers, Hans-Georg, before they might be gone and become untraceable.

My old classmate from banking school, Willi had invited us. I knew that getting a German visa for Iuu would be easy because she is my wife and we had lived together for over two years now.

We had to wait at the embassy for a good half hour. Iuu listened intensely to the interrogations the Pattaya girls had to endure before they were approved, or denied. She told me later what the questions by the Thai consular assistant were:

"How many passports have you made?" Many girls claim the old passport lost and obtain a new one so that the new boyfriend cannot see the old visas for trips to his predecessors.

"Do you have a Thai husband?" Most girls working in Pattaya or Phuket are married to a Thai husband who they either abandoned or who accepted that they are working the more lucrative sex trade servicing farang with much deeper pockets than their own.

Stories on the internet and in books recount that the Thai woman, more often than not from Isan, would egg her new farang lover on to build them a house which she can only have in her name because Thai law forbids foreign real property ownership. The farang is not aware, or not thinking, that he could simply purchase a condominium in his own name, instead, which the law permits him to have in his own name.

The woman than has the house furnished and prepared for the wedding.

Shortly before the wedding day, however, a guest with two children appears and being introduced as the long lost cousin, is welcome into the house until the farang finds out that the cousin is the Thai husband, and the children their own.

Farang suffers a broken heart, Thai woman and husband delight; end of story until the next farang appears.

Another frequently asked question:

"How many children do you have? Where are they?"

Standard reply:

"I have two children: One by my old Thai husband, and one by my former farang boyfriend. They are with my mother in Udon."

She married the "old" meaning ex Thai husband in a house marriage but never legalized it by registering at the Amphur. She had to go work in Pattaya in order to support her mother and the baby and may be because she actually enjoyed the loose life better than working on the farm or in a factory. The time window is between eighteen and thirty years, and she must be a beauty or have other features to attract her farang.

The baby from the farang is a gold mine because out of a sense of duty he keeps sending money from Europe, enough for the whole family to live on. The old farang may even be the one who keeps visiting her to see his baby, but he can only come once a year, and has no idea that she is working all year round in the old trade where he first met her.

If the visa application misrepresents the intended purpose of the visit, if the Thai lady is legally married to someone other than she is traveling with or visiting, the visa will be denied. Any hint of sex work motivation will also lead to a denial.

A good ten percent of Thailand's prostitutes are carriers of HIV, which becomes a very expensive proposition for treatment in Europe by allowing a prostitute from Pattaya to enter the country and spread the disease.

The interview can take up to fifteen minutes.

When it was our turn, Iuu and I walked up to the window, I stated my case in high German, was accepted as one, and the visa was granted in two minutes. All the official wanted to see was our official marriage certificate. Iuu already had my last name. Although I'm a Canadian, the official took me for a German and waived the visa fee. I offered to pay when she replied:

"Oh, the visa is free for members of the European Community."

During the midterm break, at the end of June, 2003, we boarded Emirates Airlines to Dubai, and then on to Frankfurt where we took an Intercity Express that rushed us to Kassel in one hour at speeds that reached two hundred kilometers an hour. Willi and his wife Anni picked us up in their Mercedes-Benz, the type of vehicle Iuu hopes to drive for herself in Thailand one day.

A "Benz" as the Thais call what is a "Mercedes" in Germany costs over 6 million baht in Thailand; twice as much as in Germany due to luxury vehicles import duties and taxes. DaimlerChrysler has an assembly plant near Rayong on the Eastern Seabord that should help lower the duty but the price is still exorbitantly high for Thais.

The only ones driving Benzes in Thailand are business owners, and most of them are Thai-Chinese who, based on family discipline and tradition, are educated, have a keen sense for opportunity, and take to money like fish to water.

The Chinese are well respected in Thailand and liked for their whiter skin, but more often then not, over the years, maintain a number of mistresses with whom they may have children. If the illegitimate child is a boy, he may even be accepted by the main wife who is usually the only one legally married to the father.

While the people of Isan prefer girls over boys being the old age pension and life insurance for the mother, Chinese prefer boys to take over their business and inherit the wealth. Daughters are married off much in the same way as in old Europe and America.

Germany was more fun than Canada the year before, and Iuu agreed. We saw my former home in Kassel when I was a teenager, went to my birthplace, Göttingen, a rather impressive well maintained medieval university town, drove to northern Germany to pick up my paintings, tasted fresh cherries from Willi's and Anni's trees, and strawberries galore that Anni turned into delicious cakes teaching Iuu who was eager to learn. Iuu made many strawberry cakes at ABAC following our return.

On the last weekend before our return flight from Zurich, Switzerland, we went to Grindelwald and stayed for two nights at the Kleine Scheidegg where I went often as a little boy growing up in Basel and Biel. We took the cog rail train up to the Jungfraujoch, marveled at the snow capped Alps and inspected the Ice Palace, sending a post card home to Nonglard from the world's highest post office 4,000 meters above sea level.

Upon returning to ABAC, I was informed that my professional management accountant program had finally been approved to be taught at ABAC's graduate school of business. Iuu and I were delighted as I was the Director Thailand for the American institute and would be making more money than by simply teaching. The program started in August and I was the core instructor, teaching the first fifteen hours for the four courses in addition to my four other sections in Managerial Accounting and International Financial Management, and on top I was giving a course at neighboring Ramkhamhaeng University on four consecutive weekends on the subject of Research Methodology for Social Sciences.

The extensive workload meant a lot more money for Iuu and me, but also took a toll on our private lives. Many times I would return home simply beat with a short fuse, easily irritable and tense, which I drowned in a couple of Singha beers while Iuu was watching her Thai movies on TV. It seemed at times that the love we enjoyed was slipping away a bit at a time as we spent less time together.

Iuu was attending weekend classes at the government's informal education course to obtain her high school diploma, the so called "Mathayom 6". A school friend of hers told Iuu that they could take courses at Ramkhamhaeng University, having passed their grade nine ("Mathayom 3"), as non-degree students. The courses they passed would later be transferred to their official transcript once they could produce their Mathayum Six. Iuu jubilated at the prospect of graduating with a university degree and said she could do it in three years. I was happy.

We talked about what faculty she should chose and decided on social studies. Iuu said then she could work for the government at the Amphur. Working at the Amphur made one an important person, small but regular pay without layoffs, and good credit at the bank to buy a house, and so on. I agreed, saying that it doesn't matter what she studied during her first two years, because the mandatory courses were almost the same including English, which she now mastered fairly well, and Mathematics that she didn't and was afraid of.

"Take only two courses, Iuu. It's enough because you are new at the university and will have to learn how to study. Taking time is okay," I advised.

On the day of enrolment, Iuu broke the news that she had registered seven courses.

She went several times a week to the other campus, called Rama II in Bang Na, and got there using our Ford Ranger feeling good about herself as an important person which she was.

The news of Iuu going to university went around quickly in Nonglard and was met by surprise and admiration. She was very happy and said:

"No one would have thought three years ago, that the farm girl Iuu with only a grade six education would finish university ahead of the other girls who went to Nonglard to get their Mathayom Six while I was working on the farm."

I was happy and proud, too, because I always believed in Iuu and know that she is a winner.

The day of reckoning came in December. Iuu passed only one of her seven courses. That course, of course, was English! I congratulated and tried to comfort her that she would simply have to go back to her books and notes and try again. She did not study much, but attempted the same exams again in March and failed. Poor, Iuu, I was truly sorry for her. She resigned herself to her fate and was thinking of giving it all up except her Sunday school at Wat Teepveela to earn her Mathayum Six. One cannot be employed in an office position, or even at a super market, without the Thai high school diploma.

"Iuu, so long as you continue even with one course, pass it and then take the next, it's fine. Take seven years to get your university degree is okay. You are only twenty-two. I didn't return to university until I was twenty-nine, and look at me know, I'm a professor."

Sometimes I called Iuu "Doctor Iuu", which made her laugh and happy, I believe.

Iuu has the great gift of reasoning, is a logical thinker, but missed the formative years of learning how to learn the basic skills such as math and physics that are taught in classes seven to ten between the ages of thirteen and sixteen, when, instead, she was kept at home learning how to plant and harvest rice, and cut sugar. She said that during those years she ran a successful business from her home making juice and the popular Thai Papaya Salad called "Samtam".

"My samtam was the best. I had a lot of customers," she said proudly, and knowing how quick and well she cooked for us at ABAC, I trusted her completely.

"I am not the type who will work in an office," she argued. "I don't like a complicated life."

She was right, absolutely right. People should do what they are good at, which does not mean in the least that they are not smart. It's just a different type of activity, and it was enough for both of us that I had the skills to make money, she had others like selling to people and talking to them that I did never, and could never, match.

We spent our Christmas vacation on my favorite Island of Koh Chang in the newly built hotel of our old hangout, Cookies, at White Sand Beach.

We arrived on December 21, 2003, were the first registered guests and got a fabulous air-conditioned room with a balcony on the second floor with a great view of the ocean right from our bed. I felt home instantly and didn't want to leave.

"We don't have to sit on the beach anymore. We can watch the ocean right from our bed."

Iuu watched her regular Thai movies in the evening while I was nursing on a couple of Singha's, and if I had any strength left, we would go out to the disco on the beach, listen to the music, or just walk hand in hand along the shore, listening to the waves, adoring the moon, and embracing and kissing each other. It was a great way to end the year. Our troubles and tensions at ABAC and Ramkhamhaeng were left behind and far away in Bangkok. My sex drive increased on a short holiday and we indulged ourselves in good eating, sleeping, and making merry.

We returned to ABAC before New Years and decided to visit Chiang Mai because Iuu had always wanted to see the city in the winter, which is actually spring by European standards, and see all the flowers in bloom. When we actually packed she wasn't so keen on traveling anymore, and it was I who said "let's go and get this behind us," which, in hindsight, I think was a mistake. Iuu hadn't told me what really bothered her until after New Years, because she didn't want to spoil our vacation.

Holding problems away from me showed Iuu's true nature. Loving and caring for others more, especially her husband, than for herself; the sacrificial Isan woman in her true nature.

"Iuu, if I would speak to you now, I would say: I know I wasn't happy at the time you broke the news and said I was disappointed that you were keeping secrets. Now I know that you actually did and meant the best."

"If I ever knew a woman who truly loved and cared, Iuu, it is YOU. I love you with all my heart. I adore and admire you for who you are. I have a wife better than anyone can ever want, wish and hope for! I need you and will guard you like the apple of my eye."

"The lessons I have learned through you are firmly planted on my mind and your test is the toughest I have ever taken in my life, adding both the fear and the pain that I must endure while the outcome is still unknown."

Chapter 9
Literature Review

A few booklets that I bought in early 2004 about Thailand including one about Isan, about "Love, Sex and Trust" in Thailand, as well as one by a British monk who lives in Thailand, contain stories that are worth reading.

Prah Peter Pannapadipo's (1997), "Phra Farang - An English Monk in Thailand" (Post Books, The Post Publishing Plc, Bangkok, ISBN 974-228-004-5) writes how people crave for situations and things they believe make them happy, and if they cannot get them suffer, but when they have them want more until they lose them and suffer again (page 19). People also crave for freedom from situations that make them unhappy. People judge us by our success or failure, but if we are lucky there comes a moment of sanity inside us saying: "Stop!"

Then we see that this competing and acquiring is basically unsatisfactory and leads nowhere. Not until then are we beginning to search for genuine meaning and understanding of our lives. For some the method is meditation, for others spiritual quest, to achieve a turning away from materialism, the pursuit of pleasure as the highest good, and society's false values.

The booklet from Günther Ruffert, "A Window to Isan", is worth noting. It is written in German entitled "Ein Fenster zum Isaan" and published by Farang Edition, Matt Publications in Banglamung (farang@loxinfo.co.th). The author worked in Thailand in the 1960s as a construction engineer. Upon retirement in 1990, he moved to a small village in Isan where he lives with his new Thai wife.

Ruffert writes about love-hungry tourists who travel to Pattaya and Phuket where the girls from Isan are waiting for them ["like grizzly bears in Alaska for the annual the salmon run" – author], and that it would save them a lot of grief and trouble to learn about the motives and customs of their new girl friends and may be wives.

Ruffert lists a few rules that the people of Isan live by and that I found to be true (pages 19-20):

(1) Isan people prefer to live in community with others,

(2) making money is more important than ethical rules,

(3) quick and easy is preferred over perfection,

(4) small talk is preferred over abstract theories,

(5) external values are more important than internal ones,

(6) the here and now is more important than the future.

Sexual morality is much stricter in the villages of Isan than what the tourist may observe in the tourist centers, writes Ruffert. Bodily contact between a man and a woman in public is taboo and feelings are not shown.

Without fun ("sanook") that is shared, life has no meaning. Any occasion is good enough to start a celebration and marriages are especially elaborate. But work is no fun ("mai sanook") and must be shared with others to allow talking and laughing.

Isan people have a passion for gambling (pages 21-23).

Children are raised much more gentle than the author, who was born a German, considers normal, but the children have a duty to care for their parents when they are grown up.

Foreigners who marry an Isan women have a hard time understanding this custom. A woman who does not care for her parents loses her face (page 29).

About a hundred years ago, Thais were ordered by way of a Royal Edict to adopt a last or family name. Before, only first names were needed. But all Thais have nicknames that they use in daily life. Such names can signify size, such as Lek (tiny), Noi (small), Nit (a little), or Yai (big). Nicknames can signify animals: Gop (frog), Kai (hen), Moo (pig), Ped (duck), Nok (bird), or Noo (mouse). (Page 37).

Morgan Lake and Kristian Schirbel (2000), "Love, $ex & Trust. Romantic Adventures in Thailand" (Phuket Co. Ltd., Phuket), worked as teachers in Thailand for many years and wrote a pocket book that is a must to read. The authors warn how foreign men who have lost their love at home and come to Thailand to heal their wounds with an enchantingly beautiful and charismatic Thai lady found more heartbreak, lost their life savings, and sometimes their lives. (Page 7)

Southeast Asia is the most densely populated region in the world, the authors say. Stepping on each other's toes is best avoided by politeness. Trustworthiness ("Wai Jai") is rare in Thailand (Pages 15). Being stingy ("kee-niow") is a deadly sin in Thailand, while laziness ('khee-giat") is accepted (page 21).

Morgan and Schirbel observe that mothers run most homes in Thailand while the father works six days a week, twelve hours a day; but many Thais have no father who left with the first pregnancy.

While girls became women, men often remain helpless mama-boys, say the authors (page 23). Thai men have a bad reputation. Farang men are preferred as boy friends and husbands because they don't leave the family or look for younger girlfriends, and provide an education for the children because they have money (page 22).

The authors believe that many girls follow the mother's role of sacrificing themselves and become bar girls in order support their family (pages 25, 26). Falling in love was considered bad taste. Romantic love was not known in Thailand until it was introduced by the movie industry in the 1960s and makes it difficult for parents to arrange marriages (pages 28, 29).

In Bangkok, in a marriage based on romance, a dowry does not need to be paid to the girl's mother. Bangkok girls do not work as bargirls who come from rural areas where love is not a prerequisite for marriage. Making "love" for money is therefore accepted by bargirls who are all from rural areas (page 31).

It is widely accepted by farang who have lived and loved in Thailand for many years, that Thai girls are not romantic. The traditional dowry is just another excuse to send money home to mother. When the money slows or runs out, it is "good bye" farang. Thai girls don't do anything for romance, only for money (page 32). Western movies make bar girls cry with the movie stars in the film as they learn that love delivers more than gold ever can, but romance is new and the girl must choose, consciously or subconsciously. Those who choose gold and money become numb and have that vacant look on their face while they dance to the rhythm in the go-go bars. The girls, however, who choose love get married and go to school to get better jobs (page 35).

Some girls who think they choose love really choose a golden cage. The relationship only lasts for a couple of months, but may last years, then like the Nightingale the woman flies free or she cannot sing for her King, as the story "The Nightingale and the Golden Cage" goes (pages 35-36).

There is a continuing struggle between romantic love and a working relationship between friends in Thailand. The struggle is within the Thai women working in the bars and the tourist industry. The farang can play a role in how they succeed with their inner struggle, and depending on how the woman is loved, her life may be changed or she will change his life (page 36).

Thai men and women never kiss in public or hug, but only go so far as holding hands, and many women (except "Iuu", of course) don't like to kiss but show their affection by cooking and washing for their husband. Making love is a part of the arrangement. She gives it to her husband the same way that he cares for her (page 39).

The Thai woman has four rooms in her heart (according to the theme, called "see hong, hua-jai"). One room is for mother and father, one for herself, and one for her husband. She does not put all of her eggs in one basket, and does not give her heart only to one person. She is more or a business-woman than her American or European counterparts, and much wiser with powerful emotions. When a Thai woman gives her husband one room, she will endure more and serve longer than a European or American woman, and her love is strong and true (page 40).

Chapter 10
The Rough Year 2004

The events that now follow are still as fresh in my mind as if they had occurred yesterday. As I recount them and write it is only June 1, 2004.

We left Bangkok early one morning a couple of days before New Years 2003 (2546 Buddhist Era), and drove straight to Chiang Mai, the "Rose of the North". It was a ten-hour journey in our Ford Ranger. I drove myself all the way, not even thinking that "Iuu" might have liked to have her hands on the wheel, too, for a while. She never mentioned it.

The countryside flew by as we sped north reaching Chiang Mai at around six o'clock in the evening and checking into an older economy class hotel near the heart of town.

We ate near the market and went to inspect the wares that were up for sale on the sidewalks, buying a Thai shirt for myself and a few souvenirs for Iuu for her parents and friends. I forgot what they were.

The next morning we drove to the famous tourist attraction northwest of the city, up a steep and curvy road to the monastery Prah That Doi Suthep where we prayed together and made offerings. Iuu bought samtam from a street vendor and joined me taking my bread, salami and beer at a shelter surrounded by lush bushes of red poinsettias that were in full bloom. Apart from those, I did not notice any flowers that we couldn't have also enjoyed at home in Bangkok.

After our picnic of sorts, we drove back to Chiang Mai and then about three hours north to Chiang Dao, looking for a small hamlet that was praised for its simplicity and vista by a tourist we had met on Koh Chang by the name of Paul who called it a must to visit, saying it was more beautiful than anything he had ever seen in his native Switzerland.

We were advised by Paul to bring our own food, water and anything else we thought we needed, as the mountain people had absolutely nothing, not even enough drinking water. It would be an exciting visit though Spartan and anything other than comfortable. We might have to sleep in our car. I took the gamble, though Iuu didn't really care for it. In her good nature, she was bent on making me happy on these vacations, so she said nothing.

"Up to you. You want to go, then go. I'm okay," would be her response.

Iuu is a master in direct and unmistakable language. A village person, she does not mince words but comes directly to the point almost in a Western way, while Thais typically beat around the bush so as to make conversation and not hurt anyone.

It took us a while to find the road that led us through dense forest into a national park, up an extremely steep and narrow but paved road until we reached the hamlet and asked for the mayor, Kuhn Nikhom.

We offered beer and cigarettes that were eagerly accepted. The children came up to me and said with curious observation: "Farang."

The view of the mountains was great but nothing of the kind Iuu had seen, and I knew, from Kleine Scheidegg near Grindelwald, let alone the Jungfrau Joch that was one of Iuu's and my highpoints on our visit to Switzerland six months earlier.

Soon after we had sat down to rest, the news of our arrival spread through the village, and Nikom proudly announced: "We have car."

He told us there was a dance festival in the valley and the whole hamlet had decided to go if we could drive them. In my stupor, I agreed. People started piling into our dual cab and whoever found space squatted on the loading deck in the back of the pickup.

The dance festival was funny. People in their traditional native north east costumes leap-stepped around a flag pole to the rhythm of two drums beaten ecstatically by two young men who were also leaping around the pole along with the dancers.

Nikhom invited us all to have supper in a barn-type of restaurant. We had beer and some spicy food. I footed the small bill.

Nikhom, who I guessed was in his forties, made both Iuu and I feel uncomfortable by constantly pointing to young underage girls, praising their beauty and how he had seduced one or the other of their kind in the past, having sex with them in the bush or the fields.

"Have you ever tried sex," he said he would ask them?

When "no" was the answer, he would press on.

"It's easy, very easy, I can show you," and off they went he said.

"There are no hard feelings." Afterwards they simply parted and went on their individual ways.

The northern girls from this poor region are known as marketable objects, sold by their parents for 400,000 baht to body massage parlors in Bangkok for life on the threat of killing the parents if they try to escape and return home. Every now and then undercover police are said to make raids on these so called "entertainment" establishments, freeing a few of the unfortunate indentured young sex slaves, ignoring the rest in return for a bribe from the owner.

The moon was full, the drumming became more ecstatic, and people were asking for rice wine, "lao khoa", and getting drunk. We left before midnight, lost the way back and ended on roads that got narrower and narrower and eventually ended in a field. Nikhom had steered us in the opposite direction. The light of the full moon showed our mountains on the other side of the valley, and by sheer luck we found a road that led to a larger one and eventually the main road back to our hamlet.

Iuu and I were bedded down in a large youth hostel type of room with running water and a toilet. We were missing nothing and slept extremely well in the cool high altitude of about 1,400 meters above sea level.

In the morning, we packed quickly and literally fled. On the scenic drive north we picked up a young couple, two students from one of the universities in Bangkok, and decided to drive them to their destination up the steepest curvy road I have ever been on in my life, so that I wonder how machines could have made it up the mountain paving the road. Our pickup spent almost an hour in low gear, engine whining and blowing out smoke that soon became blacker and blacker.

We made it after about an hour. The name of the town directly on the boarder to Myanmar was Doi Ang Khang, a perfect tourist trap, but a charming one. Iuu spotted avocadoes on the market from the local gardens. We ate a few and kept the seeds and put them into a pot on our balcony in Bangkok. They grew into seedlings within three months and are now planted on our mango farm in Nonglard.

We had a hearty lunch and then drove back the steep mountain road, again in low gear with the engine holding back the pickup, until we reached the mandarin grows in the valley.

I don't remember what happened, but Iuu got into a bad mood. I must have said something that irked her, but I forgot what it was. I remember faintly that I said something to the effect, asking why she wanted to be in every picture I took. Yes, that's what it was. She exploded, and lectured me to be nice to her. Of course, she was right. It was a stupid thing for me to remark. I wanted her in my picture because without her what would the bare countryside tell us later? Not much. I think she was also getting tired of traveling ("only see") and her problems that she was keeping from me were wearing her down.

"I'm sorry, Iuu, so sorry. Please forgive me for being unthoughtful. You didn't deserve this, my lovely wife and travel companion to wherever I wanted to go and you didn't really care for. I love you and took your love for granted. Forgive, please forgive."

Iuu's bad mood lasted another hour, then she seemed to be over it. We stopped on the way to the city of Mae Chan, still near the border to Myanmar, to rest at a park with a geyser and took photos.

Further along the road I stopped again at a native sales stand. All of the sudden the hill tribe ladies that might have slipped over the border to sell their hats and glitter, took a hold of me and just wouldn't let me go. I had to literally fight my way back to the car, plucking their arms off of mine time and again, until I could lock the door and they were still yelling at me from the outside holding up their glitter. Eventually I bought what looked like a silver necklace with a big ornament for Iuu for a hundred baht and simply took off. Iuu wasn't particularly interested in the souvenir which now hangs idle on a nail besides the mirror over the bedroom dresser. We came back to the pushy sales tactics of the mountain ladies time and again, and each time wonder how we ever got trapped so rudely.

In the later afternoon we passed through Chiang Rai, and in the evening arrived in the village of Nonglieb near Thoeng to visit Geet's parents and family, were put up in Geet's brother's house and told we could not sleep together in one bed because fucking was not allowed in his house. The brother and wife had a young daughter who was to be shielded from any sexual desires that Iuu and I might exert. Geet's brother insisted that he sleep with me, while Iuu should sleep with his wife. He gave up when he learned that Iuu and I would have none of this, and that we were too tired in any event to even think of sex.

I have never encountered demands on my private married life anywhere in the world before, and I have traveled the world several times over. The last place to expect such prudery was in Thailand, the country best known the world over for her sexual permissiveness. Iuu disagreed with me and said, for example, that Thais never kiss in public as we do in the West. The permissiveness takes place only behind closed doors. I remember having read that Thai women like to hide underneath blankets to shield their nakedness which they find embarrassing until the act actually beings and all rules and superstitions are thrown overboard.

I'm sure Iuu told Geet about this incident when she returned to Bangkok, as I later learned, Geet knew everything about Iuu's and my private life, including details of matters where I had hurt Iuu's feelings but Iuu didn't want to talk about it to me, fearing that I might get upset. I was sorry to learn this, because in my European culture the one and only person a married woman would confide in is her husband, never an outsider no matter how close as a friend.

Thai culture. It's different. Iuu had a need to share her experience with a friend she trusted, a friend who seemed to listen and to care, while I was not such a good listener, I confess. Also, women may find it easier to share their experiences with other women than with a man even if he is their husband.

The problem with the Geet-Iuu relationship was that Geet was never married, had been abandoned by her boyfriend for whom she had saved herself in expectation of marriage, and had become a pessimistic and critical spinster. I wonder what the influence of her counsel was on Iuu when the going got rough. I presume that Geet exerted an influence on Iuu to make Iuu more assertive and determined to build her own life, be that at the expense of driving me away. Because when the trouble came, Geet showed how unsympathetic and merciless she really was towards me, although we had spent a lot of time together, taking her on trips where she maintained a friendly atmosphere, though never being warm to me.

In the morning the all too familiar sound reached my ear: "We have car."

Iuu and I were hired to visit a famous Buddhist temple, a "wat", about an hour's drive away from the village. The problem was that after we left and were on the main road south, no one knew where exactly it was other than that Geet had visited it, as she had toured and inspected the whole north, and all on her own which is very untypical of the Thai way of taking a friend along for company.

The name of the famous temple we were looking for was not what was said, but Wat Ana'ayo, well marked on my Michelin map of Thailand. It was a nice place, but nothing compared to Prah Tat Doi Sutep in the hills north of Chiang Mai.

We returned on the main highway to Chiang Rai. I saw a short cut back to the village by following the map and got home to our friends in about an hour. Geet's brother had never been along the roads I took. I later learned that, as opposed to his sister Geet, he had hardly ever been outside the village except in the main city of Chiang Rai. Now I began to understand his extraordinary prudery about his proposed sleeping arrangement for Iuu and me. I'm also quite sure that he had never known any woman until he married his wife, a nice and quiet lady of his own age.

Once again, Iuu and I kind of fled the following morning, and were happy to be alone and free again. In Nonglard she often asked me to stay over and that I should return home to Bangkok alone because there was an Isan dancing festival in the Wat that she wanted to attend. Not so this time, though.

On that day, we only stopped at Sirikit Dam outside Uttaradit, reaching the city of Phitsnulok in the evening where we bedded down after visiting the local temple and having a nice dinner in a Chinese restaurant along the river.

Back in Bangkok the next evening, Iuu finally broke the news.

"Mother called and said I should come to Nonglard. Tiu is already there. I will take the bus tomorrow night and go for a few days alone."

I didn't have to guess. My direct answer to her was only one word:

"Father?"

"Yes," she replied acknowledging that the news wasn't good.

"Motorcycle accident again"? I queried.

"Again. He is severely injured and mother said I should come and see."

"When did she call? How long do you know?"

"It happened on December 20. I didn't want to tell you because it would have spoiled your vacation."

"Iuu, " I said, "I almost felt like asking you whether you wanted to drop by at home when we were in Phitsanulok last night. I had an inkling, somehow, but I didn't'. It would have been a quick shot of only a few hours. Okay, then, we will go together to Nonglard tomorrow morning. I want to drive you, not have you go alone."

I got a little upset and indignant about her being secretive and I told her so. She replied once again that she didn't want to spoil my vacation. She was right, she did her best in the circumstances being of no help in Nonglard, anyway, because father's accident was so severe that he had already spent two weeks in the hospital and had just arrived back in Nonglard after mother Tang had refused to take him back home, but Bungkert's mother had simply dropped him on her.

Iuu was once again doing her duty towards her family while trying hard, very hard, to keep me at peace. She suffered seeing that I was beginning to become critical of her family, which I have subsequently learned, is an absolute taboo in Thailand. She didn't want to hurt me, but at the same time she could also not ignore her mother's wishes, and her father's dilemma, being, as she put it, the only parents she had.

The details, as she told me, where that once again father had taken money from mother (this time he bagged the rice, sold it at the mill instead of giving it to Tang), and then disappeared not coming home at night. Driving away from the karaoke completely drunk, he drove into the ditch overturned a couple of times, and was found nearly dead by passers-by. Iuu's mother was not notified until several days later when she alerted Iuu, probably while we were on Koh Chang celebrating our well deserved and needed Christmas vacation.

I can feel the pain and turmoil that Iuu most have gone through, hurting again from what father had done to mother, wishing that he was dead while at the same time hoping for the best recovery.

"He is still my father," she had said to me when he had the motorcycle accident three months earlier. "No matter what he does."

Would I have shielded such bad news from Iuu, had they hit me, or could I have? Absolutely not. Westerners don't have that quality. We externalize our problems because we are impatient, seeking quick relief from our suffering. Iuu kept it inside for over a week while maintaining a perfect composure on the outside. I might be a poor reader of her mind and heart, and probably am, but Iuu did not show the slightest irritation, and it was not because she did not care, but because she is a master at presenting herself as the perfect wife and woman, no matter what the cost is to her internal self. She has a strength of character and mind that I have never ever seen in anyone. I hurt knowing that she suffered only to remain gentle and kind to me without demanding anything for herself. I hurt because I have not treated her with the same consideration and kindness that she, unbeknownst to me, was treating me.

I begin to understand myself, why I reached the conclusion several months ago that I was beginning to become unfit to return to my native Europe or North America to resume a life there, even if Iuu comes with me.

The down to earth truth is that I do not find Western ways, faces and whatever else we have, attractive enough anymore to compensate for any loss of the simplicity, directness, tenderness of the Thai soul, and willingness to sacrifice her ego only to keep harm from her loved ones including myself, as does my Isan wife, Iuu.

I understand perfectly now her conclusion that if she ever marries again it will only be for money, not love, because love of her husband, and for her family has brought joy, yes, but at the price of more grief.

Iuu, I say to you:

Now I know, having emphasized my thoughts by the written word, why you are respected as the *numero uno*, the number one person in your family and even among your extended family, your cousins. You have gone up to the plate and sacrificed for them when no one else could or would. You were only eighteen, of tender age, when mother was penniless. You did not hesitate to step up to the plate by offering yourself, body and soul, to pull your family out of misery by marrying yourself to a man you absolutely did not love. You did so because it was the only immediate, sure way out of your family's problems that was open to you. You had no skills, no job to earn the money that was needed. How else could you have done it? You could not.

You shook off the burden at the first opportunity when you were not appreciated by him. I don't blame you in the least.

When the money was gone and no one else could provide, father having just been released from jail, you went to Pattaya to sacrifice yourself again and by providing pleasure to men you also did not love or care for in order to send money home and ease your loved one's burden. You are fun loving, too, like you should be, but not a party girl, one who enjoys the bar scene. I saw only a faint courteous smile on your lips when we first met at Marine Disco in Pattaya on that night from May 26 to 27, 2001.

Iuu, I told you many times that I knew you from the minute I first saw you. I did not spend the night with you because I was horny, and neither did you. In fact I was dead tired, but seeing and recognizing you, I could not pass you up, was allowed to hold you in my arms all night long, although you could have made our meeting just an hour's affair. I fell in love with you deeply during our first innocent night together. It was so fulfilling to have found you at last after my nine years of abstinence following the divorce from my wife number two.

Iuu, you told me later, actually only one month ago over that impersonal telephone that left me no chance to respond:"

"Michael, you always put me down. I am not good enough for you. All men are like this."

Yes, I have cried and sometimes still cry over you.

You are right, Iuu, and you are wrong also. This man, myself, does not want to be like you said men are, even if he was or might have been. This man has learned the lessons you have taught him, finally, and well. Now you must become free yourself by forgiving me if you care as I know you do. I never intended to hurt you.

A lot in our life together is and was circumstance over which we have no control, or lost control. Please judge me by my intentions, not by inadvertent and unintended actions and their result. If you condemn and not forgive, you will find it hard to love again, and without allowing those who truly love you to show their love and affection to you, you will hurt more and no longer be Iuu, who we all love.

Chapter 11
Enduring Her Father

Leaving Bangkok at around noon after a short night's rest, washing a few things, and packing anew, we made it to Udon Thani late at night and decided to stay in the hotel where I had waited for "Iuu" nearly three years earlier and drive to Nonglard the following morning. We were tired and beat, dropped into bed and passed out.

We came prepared but Bungkert's appearance still shocked us. He greeted us with a faint "hello", and just sat there on a cushion on the concrete living room floor, moaning in pain from time to time.

"Car accident," he said to me without any expression on his face. His left eye was wide open with a bruise on the eyebrow. His right eye looked serious but normal. His left arm was in a cast, as was his right leg right up to the hip, and his left leg up to his kneed. He wore a light red jacket and had a cigarette in his hand. His lower lip was bruised. We later saw the motorcycle at his mother's house a few kilometers outside Udon Thani and loaded it onto our pickup truck. Many people saw it when we took it back to Bangkok and asked in deep sympathy whether the driver was dead.

"He lives," replied Iuu., "He's my father."

The inquirers asked no more, and silently went away. I am always amazed how direct and open Isan folks are about private and often troublesome matters. They must have a need for communication, even if things are unpleasant. It's an open contradiction to the habit of keeping bad things to themselves and inside.

Squatting beside Bungkert was his mother, Iuu's grandmother. She had brought her son two days before our arrival and simply dropped him on his wife, Tang, who had refused to take him back but now had no choice. I knew Iuu's paternal grandmother from our visit to her several months ago. I wanted to meet her, and Bungkert who hadn't seen her for almost a decade, and Tang, came along to say hello and spent a few hours together, eating, and talking.

Bungkert looked a lot like his mother, but she did not have the savage wildness in her face as Bungkert did. She appeared like a farm woman who had worked hard all her life to sustain her family, and had a somber and solemn expression on her face. She spoke little or nothing, looking very concerned, checking on Bungkert from time to time by rearranging his clothes or doing this or that.

Iuu's mother, Tang, also said nothing. May be a few words to Iuu, now and then, spoken quietly almost in a whisper.

Tiu was said to be in the village. We didn't see him until the evening when his friend on a motorcycle dropped him off. He joined the family for dinner and then left again.

Bungkert had a very restless night. At one time, I heard flesh hitting flesh and woke Iuu up and told her what I had heard, asking whether mother was trying to kill father.

"He is trying to kill her," she replied, already aware of the situation. "He tells her to not fall asleep but to watch over him at all times. How can she do that? I would like to knock out the bastard. He should have died in the accident."

The next day, Iuu said to me that she had done her duty and was ready to go home to Bangkok and told her mother that she did not intend to return to her troubled home in Nonglard unless someone died to attend the "funeral" party.

I guess mother asked her to stay over another day, and to drive Bungkert to the clinic to have his dressing changed. Iuu obliged. We took Bungkert to the clinic every day, including the third day of our departure, taking the motorcycle home with us to Bangkok. Iuu wrapped it in a big sheet of blue plastic to make sure it couldn't be seen by anyone. It was an embarrassment to her.

I had a class on the following day, the next term of my professional accounting program began, and life resumed as usual.

During the months of January to April, 2004, I had three sections to teach at ABAC, in addition to the five weeks of professional accounting all Saturday and Sunday, for which I was the Director and also the core instructor. In mid-February, another four weeks of teaching at Ramkhamhaeng University began, also all day Saturday and Sunday. Our Dean, Brother Vinai, had been let go in November, and was replaced by a young Thai professor who had been elevated to the position of Chairman of the Academic

Committee, firing people, deleting courses including my international financial management course, and gave the faculty outside his inner circle nothing but grief by making orders behind closed doors.

The man began attacking my professional accounting program by demanding documents, asking questions, and calling me for meetings at moment's notice which I refused to attend unless I had prior notice of the agenda in order to prepare and respond properly. His intention was to have my program squashed and struck from the calendar because he said, that being a professional program from the outside, it had no place in the halls of academic learning. The truth was that he could not be a part of it because he was not qualified, and my program had doubled in student attendance from ten going for the final examination to twenty in only one term, blocking four other electives and eliminating the thesis option, taking away the lucrative income of the so called thesis advisors and their examiners.

My weekend teaching at Ramkhamhaeng University was completed in mid-March. At about the same time, supported with all kinds of ammunition, two of my former students from the professional accounting program where making an official complaint that the certificate they had earned was not the one they had expected and demanded their money back for the entire course fee.

There were several hearings before the Vice President for Academic Affairs, a Brother of the Order of St. Gabriel, during which I was asked to answer and submit documents in defense of the university and my program. Questions to answers led to more questions. At about the same time, another American Institute began its inquiry through our course material supplier in the United States. Our tightly nit circle in Washington responded advising to back off, and the publisher did.

But in March, the other institute filed a law suit in Federal Court, and a complaint before the Internet arbitration board to have the domain for our website transferred to them for the alleged violation of their U.S. trademarks that had in fact been abandoned in 1995. I knew they could win by playing poker with legal fees we could not afford and going for default judgment.

This very American way of bullying the rest of the world not for what we do in America but in Asia, and the U.S. courts' willingness to exercise extraterritorial jurisdiction over other nations, left a very foul taste in my mouth. As Canadians looking in, we generally know more about the United States than the average American himself, can do business and visit any time we like, but have the advantage of leaving by simply crossing their northern border back into safe and civilized Canada.

My colleagues in Washington asked me to draft a response as the activities of the institute at the time were entirely concentrated in Thailand. On March 21, 2004, I received notice from the Human Resources Department at ABAC, that my contract would not be renewed and that I would be leaving the university at the end of April.

I told Iuu about my dismissal the same day. She was devastated wondering where we are going to live, and started to worry. Then she said we could always move into the Interplace Hotel down the street where many other professors had moved to get away from the fish bowl of ABAC Hotel.

"What are we going to do, " she asked. "Where are we going to live."

"I have been in these kind of situations before, Iuu," I replied calmly almost not caring. "There is always a place we can go to. Don't worry."

That answer did not satisfy Iuu, but she said nothing. The next day after work she sat in the arm chair and said directly to my face:

"I am worried. I don't like this. Can we stay in Bangkok for another year until I have completed my Mathayum Six"?

"You can get a high school diploma anywhere, Iuu, not only in Bangkok."

Once again my reply was not satisfying, but she said nothing. I was right because I knew, but she did not and, I believe, began to doubt me.

Iuu began asking me little questions whose importance I did not realize until much later when I came to think about them. For example, she said one evening:

"Can you buy me silver? I found a nice necklace and bracelet for only 1,400 baht?"

Again I replied negatively, saying that we better wait until I had a new job and we knew where we are going.

"I will go with you wherever you go," she replied and made me feel comfortable, although now I believe she was not comfortable and continued to worry abut our future. What I should have told her was, that I had worked so hard during the last term in this one, that we had four hundred thousand baht in cash in the bank, but I didn't tell her. I was wrongfully concerned that if I did, she would ask to build a house for mother and father now that we had the money. I now don't believe that she would have done so, but been prudent enough to wait and see. We had enough money to buy her the small amount of silver, and I fail to understand why I was such a hard ass to put it off.

Small gifts, every now and then, go a long way for establishing and maintaining a good relationship. I think I was both overworked from the intense course load, and felt down by the problems of my dismissal, the problems with the accounting program, and the two legal actions against my institute in the United States.

Iuu's next test question that I failed to identify as such was whether she could build an additional room to her mother's house that was now in her name. We had gone to Nonglard on March 8, 2004, to pay off a loan mother had taken out at father's urging against the house a year ago, and if it wasn't paid off the bank might initiate proceedings against the mother to force repayment. I agreed to pay the money on condition that mother transferred the title to the house to Iuu, so that it would be out of father's reach to have another lien made against it to raise money for him to spend.

The month of March was a disaster month all around. On the 27th of March, Iuu and I wanted to escape to Koh Chang for a few day's rest and to refresh our relationship, have some fun at the beach, eat and sleep well, and have sex together for which a short vacation always seemed the precisely right medicine. Not that we didn't do it at home, but it was an added stimulus.

Just before we made it to the motorway, Geet made her routine daily call to Iuu, and when she learned we were off to Koh

Chang asked whether she could join us. I refused out of hand and Iuu told Geet so. Then, with hindsight, knowing how Iuu enjoyed having a friend with her to converse in Thai, I changed my mind and agreed. We drove the car in search of a U-turn, which took a good ten minutes, and then picked up Geet who was standing outside her barber shop packed already to go.

The weekend in Koh Change with Geet not parting from Iuu and giving Iuu and me the space I desired, became a nightmare that added to the irritation I was already under. The four-hour journey was okay. On arrival at Cookies Hotel where we had reserved a room, Geet made no motion to look for her own hotel because ours was on the high side, Iuu knowing how stingy Geet was and hard to part with her money. So, it was decided to put Geet up in our room to share the big King size bed. What an idiotic idea. It was Geet not only during the entire day, but whole night as well.

I can hide my displeasure for a while, but not as well and for so long as Iuu had done during our Christmas vacation on Koh Chang.

One evening Iuu said she would go downstairs with Geet to see what was going on. Three hours later, half past midnight, they were still out. I went looking for them and couldn't find them, then went back into our room and security-locked the door, intent on having them sleep in the car. Then I called Geet on her cell phone because Iuu had left hers in the room. Iuu answered me and said they were drinking on the other end of the beach and having a good time, but she would be coming home now.

When the door rattled and Iuu demanded entrance, saying: "Open Michael, open. Don't make a problem. Open," I got up and opened the door. The two came in as if they had never left, and we all went to bed. We stayed only for two nights, and after discounting the travel time, the trip was hardly worth it.

Geet decided to tell me: "Now I know you," Iuu translating the Thai words into English. I believe it meant so much as that I wasn't the kind of character she had anticipated. I'm not sure why she said it, because Iuu and I had taken Geet along on day trips, and one weekend to Koh Samed where she stayed only one night and returned back to her barbershop, both to save money and to make money.

"Geet is kiniow (meaning "stingy")," said Iuu. I wondered why she still went to see and phone her on an almost daily basis. Iuu could have had many friends of her own interests, including married ones, but she didn't. On several occasions the thought arose in me that Geet might be a lesbian and was attracted to Iuu who said she was a little bit Tom. Geet lived together wilth a girl from the mountains from Chaing Rai Province, but had never married.

A man from the room next door on Koh Chang, an Indian man with a Thai mother as he explained, spoke to her, and later called her up to meet her, but Geet, going out together with him decided that he was not her type and only wanted to have sex with her which she declined she told Iuu.

The man had taken both Geet, the Little Girl (Geet's companion), and Iuu out for dinner. When I called Iuu around seven she told me she was with Geet. When I called again at nine, she said she was coming home now. And when I called again at eleven at night asking what held her up, Iuu replied there was a motorcycle accident but she would be home any minute now. Iuu came back shortly before midnight and said she had been out with Geet, the Little Girl and the man for dinner.

"There was no motor cycle accident," I said. "I checked and the Soi Ramkhamhaeng was clear."

"You are right. I but I had to say something to you," she explained.

"So you lied," I complained. "Please don't lie to me anymore and tell me if you are going somewhere."

"You wouldn't have liked it, so I told you nothing. Now I'm here," she replied convinced that she was right.

I didn't like what she said, but put the matter to rest, happy to have her home now. Married to a young woman, I thought to myself, I have to roll with the punches. No choice.

During the last week of March there was no let up at ABAC. More meetings with the two rebellious Chinese students, and then ABAC's refusal to honor the institute's bill for 360,000 baht, not releasing the institute's program fee collected by ABAC from the twenty students in my professional accounting program. I had advanced the costs of the 104 books I had ordered at the commencement of the term, incurred other expenses, got the students to sign evaluations and requests to release their funds to the institute, but ABAC responded with silence.

I let Iuu know of the impasse, which was probably not a wise thing to do given the other problems including ABAC's notice of termination of my employment (which reversed on April 19th). The window of time left to find a new position was getting narrower, but I had no time to become active because my courses were still running, and the two American law suits demanded my input by way of detailed responses to the points that were raised in the two complaints.

The institute had not yet hired a lawyer, and when they did I had to transfer the remaining funds from its bank account in Bangkok to pay for the retainer.

I still had about 465,000 baht cash in my personal bank account, but I didn't tell Iuu who might have felt that I am living on borrowed time.

On the first weekend in April, on April 2nd, 2004, I found this email in my mailbox that Iuu had sent me from her laptop. She had taken computer classes at EEC and was teaching herself by experimenting. She wrote me sweet messages often, adding pictures to make them look nice, and I responded with a few words of thanks and appreciation, telling her that I missed her, too, although sometimes she was sitting in the room with me, and replying by saying that I loved her.

I suggested to Iuu, and she agreed, that we escape to Koh Samed for two nights, which would give us one clear day of spending quality time together to make up for the lost weekend on Koh Chang. We would go alone, just her and me.

I was happy. I think we had a good time. Iuu made every effort to make me happy, hugged and kissed me, made love, and even agreed to swim with me in the ocean which she did not actually like, and hike up the mountain for exercise that she despised.

We stayed up late taking a few drinks and danced at the disco on Silver Sand Beach where we stayed. Iuu wanted to drink and dance and be happy. I went along as good as I could, but somehow couldn't shake myself loose from my worries and join her in having complete fun. There was a full moon at night that turned me on. I talked to Iuu how she had turned me on two years earlier, doing it with me in the ocean at Laem Mae Ping, and then again on Koh Chang. Would she have me tonight in the ocean again.

"How about some sweet romance in the moonlight," I asked curiously.

"People might see us," she objected. "I don't like. We have the room."

"Okay, the room."

Then Iuu brought another couple of test questions forward that only upon reflection I identified as such, but missed entirely when she posed them.

"I have a baby I didn't tell you about," she said as we were strolling along the beach in the beautiful moonlight.

"Really?" I said with surprise. "Who is the father?"

"I don't have to tell you everything," she answered.

"Do you know? Is he an older man, or same age?"

"I don't have to tell you," she replied once again.

"Is it a boy or girl. What happened to the baby?"

"It's a boy. He is with his father," she said. "What do you think about me now that I tell you?"

I didn't even think about it first before I gave a reply, and said instantly, giving her back in kind:

"I don't think I want to live with you anymore," and then adding immediately thereafter. "Come on, Iuu, I think you are making this up. I don't believe any of it. If you already have a baby, you would have had another one or two, by me, but you don't."

Iuu started laughing and leaned on me, hugging me slightly: "Yes, I made it up just to test you."

Iuu was never boring, I thought. What a character, making up stories just to entertain me. But I missed the point. Iuu was troubled by my troubles at ABAC and perhaps was wondering, how would Michael respond if I had a problem. Would he be understanding, trying to help me, or would he turn away. Although she laughed that she had made up the story, I believe she got the answer to her question, and the answer was not good. I was stupid, because I only wanted to pay her back for keeping a secret for so long, and would never leave Iuu because she already had a baby but rather welcome it if the father released it to her.

That wasn't the end of her stories.

"I have killed my baby," she said.

"What, you killed your baby, and the police let you go free?" I replied half joking now, and half serious. I didn't know what to think.

"The police don't know about it. I killed it in my stomach," she asserted putting on a serious face.

Then she said, that was just another story and there was no truth to it, but that next weekend I should fuck her a lot because she would be receptive. She counted out the days from her period that had just ended and confirmed:

"Next weekend, we can try again."

I embraced and kissed her and said something to the effect: "Will do."

Then we returned to the disco and danced a while until we turned in for a little intimacy and fell asleep until the morning.

We returned to ABAC on Monday evening, April 5th and I remember in the morning lay together intimately in each other's arms, feeling completely united and peaceful. I thought to myself we should sleep like this all the time. When sometimes we did, Iuu would tell me proudly: "We slept all night together" and was happy.

On Tuesday, April 6th, I had only a week left to file the internet dispute response in the United States, and decided to finish it all that same day to be rid of it. I had formulated the response in my mind during the weekend with Iuu on Koh Chang and was ready. In the back of my mind, though, I had the thought of simply leaving it for another day, because people who overwork to win in business often lost their wives in the process. I dismissed the thought.

Chapter 12
Troubled Waters

This chapter describing the events on the evening of Tuesday, April 6th, 2004, is one of the hardest to write.

We woke up at about six thirty in the morning. After returning from the bathroom going back to bed, "Iuu" came over to me and we cuddled together naked as we were, embracing each other tight and fell asleep for another hour or so. It felt so good having her so firmly in my arms and close to me, and I believe she felt the same way.

We didn't make love. She usually wasn't open in the morning and had no craving for sex. I had said to her many times that sex was not the most important thing in my life, but rather living with her and being bonded to each other was first and foremost in my heart and mind and mattered a lot more than sex.

She would reply: "I don't believe you, Michael. I think you like sex a lot."

"Yes, I like sex a lot, too," I would reply. "But only you. I don't have eyes for anyone else."

"I know," she replied. "I know. Sometimes on the street you don't even notice me."

It happened that I came out of the elevator at our ABAC Hotel at the lobby while she was waiting to get in and called my name because I hadn't noticed her. She thought it was funny, but she also knew perfectly well that I was faithful both in thought and deed, and wouldn't even look at other women because I loved only Iuu, fully and completely.

We took showers, made coffee and smoked a cigarette. Then I watered the plants on our balcony. I had brought them to act as a shield against the height of our twelfth floor because I didn't like Iuu to step up to the balcony wall, looking down and feeling scared as she did when she first moved in. We had a banana tree, a coconut that we had brought from Koh Chang during our first visit, a small coconut also from Koh Chang that we picked from the eastern shore on our Christmas vacation, a few other plants, and two trays mounted on the outside balcony wall containing a cactus, a small orange tree and herbs, and a hanging pot containing flowers Iuu had brought from Nonglard and was pruning on a regular basis.

While I readied myself to finish the internet dispute response on my computer, Iuu did some odd chores around the room, then came up to kiss me on the cheek, saying she was going to see Geet.

"Okay, you can take the car. I'm busy at home all day."

"I will call you," she said and left.

The problem was that Iuu didn't have a job other than preparing for exams a couple of days before she had to sit for them, wasn't really doing anything to occupy herself. From time to time she suggested to take a job in order to be busy and independent of my allowances, and so that she could send money home to mother when she wished. My reply was that I didn't want Iuu to help other people get rich by underpaying her.

"I don't like my wife to work for one hundred fifty baht a day. It's peanuts. I give you more in weekly allowance and pay mother, too."

"But then it's my money. I don't care if it's small," was her answer.

The idea of Iuu seeing Geet every other day, or even daily, irked me. I didn't like it, especially after our Koh Chang vacation a week before, but what else could I suggest? There was another woman in our life who had a completely different agenda and with whom Iuu, I thought, had nothing in common. Geet was a loner who didn't want to be married, may even reject men, I thought, while Iuu was a young energetic woman with a future but was not working on it.

Iuu had booked a course at EEC Learning Center on Ramkhamhaeg Road across from The Mall. I later learned that she had not attended several classes. Perhaps she had forgotten.

I worked all day on the computer, checking the complaint, answering each point meticulously, comparing previous decisions, including the relevant legal issues in my argument. The only idea in my mind was to finish the response, send it off, and be rid of it. It was very intense hard work and the hours just flew by. I was so occupied that I forgot about lunch.

At around four o'clock in the afternoon I was done. I saved the word document to disk and shut down the computer. Then I went to the fridge, found a full Singha beer, opened it and clicked on the TV to watch the news on CNN and the BBC.

Iuu called.

"I'm at Big C. Can I bring you anything?" she asked.

"I don't know, Iuu. I think we have everything?" I replied.

"How about some beer. Do you want salami and bread?"

"Sure, whatever you think, I'll appreciate it."

"Okay, see you in a couple of minutes. Bye," Iuu said and hung up.

She arrived in our room around five o'clock, dropped the shopping bags and hugged and kissed me as she always would. Then she sat down in the armchair and relaxed. We didn't talk about anything in particular that I remember.

She had brought three large beers. One Heineken and two Singhas. I put them into the fridge, which was now full. I had already finished one beer and was now opening the second, and half an hour later the third, while munching on the bread and salami Iuu had brought me. She had also brought a small bag of fish balls for herself to eat.

I don't remember that Iuu, sitting in the armchair actually did anything. She seemed quiet, I believe. She might have had some talk with Geet about us leaving ABAC, about her desire to finish her Mathayom Six, about our relationship, or whatever. I don't know what Geet's answer might have been, but I knew Geet's influence on my young wife's mind was an important one, and one that I could not ignore. The problem was that Geet spoke no English, could not tell me anything, and I could not ask her any questions.

I now know that Geet thinks that I am not treating Iuu right. That I am easy to anger and turn a small matter into a big problem, that I cannot change, and that Iuu is stuck unless she frees herself. This came out in long talks between Geet and me a month later with a new Thai friend of mine translating. I also knew that Geet did not hold men in any particular regard, perhaps, including me. That she liked if not loved my wife, Iuu, and wanted Iuu around herself as much as she could. I don't want to pass blame on Geet. Perhaps she was neutral all in all, only enjoyed Iuu's company, and vice versa. Whatever happened minutes later were my and Iuu's actions, and only ours.

All of a sudden there was a bang and the sound of glass breaking. I turned and looked at Iuu. She was startled. The ABAC clock on the wall above the dresser had fallen down and smashed the wine glass below, the only one left that I rinsed myself. Iuu and I looked at each other. I believe she said:

"Bad thing happening."

Iuu believed in ghosts and I think knew she believed we had one in our room with bad intentions. I kind of shrugged it off, but with hindsight that was a mistake. I should have talked about it with my wife, or if not about ghosts, asked her how her day went and spent time with her together. Instead I turned back to the TV watching the news that came out of Iraq, the bombings and that crap.

Everything thereafter happened very quickly, and with devastating results while I was getting somewhat drunk from the rapid consumption of beer just to overcome the stress that had built up during the day of intense work on the computer.

I got thirsty from the two and half beers that I had consumed within the last hour, reached for the water bottle in the fridge but it was empty. There was no water left in the larger bottle outside, either.

"Iuu, " I said, turning to her in the armchair, "we have not water. Can you get some?" I asked.

"No," Iuu responded. "I got the water last time, remember. Now you get it." She said it with a stern voice and not a kind tone.

"Iuu, I have no clothes on. You are dressed. Can you get the water, please?" I tried to reason with her.

"No," she responded. "You get it."

Normally, I would simply get up, make some remark to Iuu like "no woman no pain", and just go and get the water from the dispenser on the eighth floor of our ABAC Hotel. We had two elevators. It was easy, and sometimes I did so during the night when we were thirsty and had nothing to drink.

Instead, however, my drunken ego started balking, thinking, "poor me" who has worked all day while she only visited Geet talking… Then I grabbed her bag of fish balls and flung it onto the balcony.

Iuu, always quick in response, grabbed the bowl on the dresser in front of her and smashed it against the wall.

I believe in hindsight, that Iuu had not come home in a happy mood, was mulling over a lot of things in her mind, but wasn't up to talking to me about it. I hadn't told her that we had four hundred and sixty-five thousand baht cash in the bank, more than we had ever had before, and that she should be at ease and not worry. I had mentioned that we could spend a few weeks in Nonglard following Songkarn. I said I was free from the 9th of April, the day on which we could go. She wanted to go to Nonglard, though a month earlier she had said that she wouldn't go back until someone died. I had also noticed the day before that Iuu was talking nicely on the phone and asked her when she hung up who that person was.

"My father," she replied.

"Good," I had said.

The dish she had grabbed in response to my flinging her fish balls cracked against the wall and broke.

In an instant and quick reaction I grabbed her Nokia that was lying on the dresser, went to the balcony and said:

"Are you getting the water, now? One, two, three."

She looked at me with a stoic face, staring me down, saying nothing.

I counted again:

"One," waiting a second. No response from Iuu.

"Two," waiting a second. Still no response from Iuu.

"Three," hesitation. Again no response from Iuu except a stare at me.

Then, hesitating a split second again, I lifted her Nokia into the flower tray on the outer balcony wall, but when I looked I didn't see it, so it must have gone over and fell down the twelve floors to the ground.

I didn't know what to do or say in my stupor, so I just sat on the bed saying nothing.

Iuu got up and tried to go on the balcony, but I blocked the way being afraid she might do something else other than look. She sat down again in the armchair in silence for a minute while the TV kept on reporting the news on the BBC.

The problem was, and now the memory came back into my mind in a flash, about a year and a half before, she was talking on the mobile in our room for a long time and went outside when I asked her to stop. She kept on talking and talking outside in the hall by the window when I had gone to her, grabbed her Nokia while she was holding on to it, when it slipped out of our hands and fell down onto the parking lot. She had packed and stayed overnight at Geet's calling me in the morning that I could pick her up if I promised to buy her a new Nokia which I did. Many apologies and matter settled. This now was the second such incident.

After about a minute of silence, Iuu rose, went to the ward robe, got out her green traveling bag and backpack and started packing.

"I also destroy things when I'm angry," she said to me, "but only glasses and stuff but never anything of value."

"I still love you, Iuu," I pleaded. "I can buy you a new Nokia. I'm sorry."

No response, Iuu kept on packing underwear, bras, shirts, went to her office area and took some papers including the land card for the mango farm while I watched in my stupor. Had I not been drunk, I would have tried to embrace her, offer my apologies, get dressed myself and gone with her to Big C to buy her a Nokia right there and then. But I didn't.

Instead I reached for my wallet and handed Iuu all the cash that I had, two thousand baht, saying:

"I don't want you to be without money."

Iuu looked at me somewhat puzzled, then said:

"Thank you. I always take money," and put it into her wallet.

When she was about to leave, I took the two bath (one ounce) gold chain from my drawer, flung an Isan loincloth around my waste and followed her to the elevator. I asked to kiss her, but she said: "No."

Then I put the gold chain around her neck, which she allowed me to do. She let me kiss her on the cheek. The elevator came and she was gone.

When I went back into our room it hit me like a ton of bricks that had dropped on my back. Then I saw that she had put her room and car keys on the dresser as if she wanted to say that she didn't need them anymore.

It had all happened in about five minutes. I sat down and contemplated the situation, then I got dressed and drove to Geet, assuming to find her there and talk to her. Geet was talking on the telephone for a long time and then told me using sign language and the odd English word, that Iuu had called from a public pay phone to say she had left me because I had destroyed her Nokia and not said that I was sorry.

Geet had said that she had asked Iuu: "Where are you going, and what are you going to do?"

Iuu had answered: "I don't know."

"Come here, then." Geet had offered.

"I don't want to bother you with my problems," Iuu had responded.

Then I drove to the Ekkamai Eastern Bus terminal from where the buses leave to Pattaya because my heart told me that's where Iuu would go.

There was a full bus to Pattaya about ready to leave. The luggage compartment was still open and I spotted a green bag exactly like Iuu's. I went inside the bus but Iuu was not in it. A lady came out of the washroom to take her seat, but she wasn't Iuu.

I went home devastated and deeply depressed. I don't think I slept at all except for an hour or two in the morning from sheer exhaustion. When I woke up my head felt electric, my heart hurt and hurt and hurt, and I started to sob and eventually cry for a good five minutes because I knew Iuu, how determined she was when she decided on something and that to get her back home again wasn't going to be a piece of cake, especially since I didn't even know where she was. She had gone into hiding. I remembered that she had told me once:

"If I leave you, I go somewhere where you cannot find me."

All these thoughts came back into my mind and I began to curse myself in the pain of her absence.

I had loved her deep in my heart very intensely and didn't understand why I had reacted to a stupid thing like water, or why she hadn't simply gone to get it.

"What is wrong with me," I lamented. "I quarrel with the one person I love the most, my wife Iuu. Why, why, why?"

It is a lot easier to leave someone than being left behind. She knew at all times where to find me, could call me anytime. I didn't.

I did not think that "Iuu" was leaving for good until I saw that she had left her room and car keys behind in the room that now felt so empty without her. The feeling of my soul mate having left was utter desolation and trauma. Minutes after she had left, she had called Geet to tell her about it, saying that she didn't know where to go. Hearing about it made me sad, wanting to offer anything to make her return, but I knew how stubborn she was, how determined to win rather than give in which might be seen as a point of weakness. Her willingness to suffer was the flip coin of her eagerness to delight.

I got dressed in a hurry and began searching for her, first driving to Geet and then to the Ekkamai bus station. No Iuu in sight. Then I drove home and the first of two months' of short and restless nights began. Every time I woke up, realizing the new reality, my brain felt electrically charged, the comfort of her presence gone, replaced by depression and paranoia mixed by hope and despair.

We had planned to drive to Nonglard for the Songkarn holidays, on Friday, April 9th, my first day off before the final examinations at ABAC. On the following day, April 7th, I sent messages to Iuu's parents' number saying that I loved her, and hoping that she would enjoy herself.

"Love you lan baht." (Love you a million baht.)

"Wish you sanook, sanook." (Wish you fun, fun.) A message I sent against my own disposition, trying to save face.

I was delighted when the messages were returned with the same text that I had sent. I figured everything would be alright once I got to Nonglard and saw Iuu face to face.

The following day, I called Mayor Sompong of Nonglard to inquire whether Iuu had already arrived. He checked with her parents and called back:

"Iuu is not in Nonglard. Her parents do not know where she is." My heart sank. Who had returned my mobile phone messages?

Was it a hoax by her father Bungkert? But Bungkert was mobile illiterate and could not even add money from a phone card onto a mobile number.

On Friday, April 9th, I left Bangkok around eight o'clock in the morning and sped North on the freeway to Udon Thani, arriving in Nonglard at around three in the afternoon. As I pulled up into the mud driveway, father Bungkert was resting in the hammock and mother Tang was busy raising the ground in front of the house by shoveling dirt into buckets and spreading it about. She stopped her work as I stepped out of the car and greeted me with a smile:

"Hello, Michael."

Bungkert, too, smiled at me vaguely, as he always did: "Hello, Michael."

The welcome was the usual one, except that the parents seemed to know what had happened because they did not ask, "where is Iuu?" which would be normal if I had arrived solo unannounced. Only one time had I arrived alone, which was when Iuu had gone to Pattaya with her cousin Kay in November 2002, a year and a half ago. The family and cousins where all upset, inquiring, but not this time.

I went into the house and dropped my bag in the living room, then rushed up the stairs and found the door to our room open but no bag of Iuu or other sign that she might have arrived. I went downstairs again, and set down next to Bungkert and Tang.

"Where is Iuu?" I asked.

"Don't know," answered Bungkert looking puzzled and resigned.

"Has she telephoned?"

"No telephone. Don't know," answered Bungkert.

I then began to explain what had happened, that Iuu had left two days earlier, that we had planned to come to Nonglard for Songkarn, and that I had hoped to find her here.

Bungkert replied that cousin Rin and Tao where coming tomorrow from Ban Pakong south of Bangkok, and that Iuu might come with them. The spirit of hope made me happy, and I began to relax somewhat trusting in good fortune, knowing I had done the right thing to come to Nonglard. Still, I was so depressed that I couldn't eat, and sleeping on the mattresses in our room that Tang had prepared for me, was difficult and uneasy, the only comfort coming from the feeling that I was in Iuu's surroundings where she had grown up since she was a baby.

Songkran in Northeast Thailand can be cool if the Monsoon rains arrive early which they rarely do. I had lost about ten kilograms by now, was not really eating, and as a result the otherwise unbearable heat of up to forty degrees inside the house didn't affect me as much, except that I was sweating while the locals didn't. It cooled down at night just enough to be comfortable with a running fan to sleep, but my sleep was not a wholesome one anyway. The dogs were barking all night, the roosters cried at the misconception that it might be light as early as three o'clock in the morning, and the loudspeakers with their public announcements made any rest after seven illusionary.

These reasons were among the ones why I didn't particularly like Nonglard, apart from the constant problems the family presented regarding father's running to the Karaokes and his mistresses, the need for money for hospitals, the failed rice business that proved just another rip off, and the general attitude "we don't care" (not to be mistaken for "sabai, sabai" meaning "don't worry") that seemed to prevail.

This time, however, I took a new interest in Nonglard, and began to accept the parent's simple ways because they were the producers of my missing love object, Iuu, and that everything actually was okay if only she would show up. Attitude and perception creates the truth. It his how we think about something before the thoughts become words, and the words become actions, that make it what it is.

All these days, and throughout the following two months, my emotions would overcome me until I could not hold them back anymore letting it all out. The pillow got wet, but I felt a little relieved and better afterwards, though not for long. Time and again I replayed the last five minutes with Iuu on this late afternoon of April 6th during which it all happened so quickly, banging my hand against my head. Why, Michael, why, why did you take that damn Nokia and drop it? Why, knowing Iuu's quick reactions... her boom-boom ways of doing anything if she was angry, and her stubbornness of resisting amends.

I talked to Bungkert as best I could as his English was quite weak, and told him exactly what had happened. He thought the Nokia was not a big deal, and that Iuu was easy to anger but would also forget quickly. Bungkert said Iuu would be back, only as to the timing he said he didn't know. I asked Tang several times whether Iuu had called her, and each time she replied: "No." I even asked her to look at me and say it again, which she did, and again she replied: "No."

I now know that Tang was lying. She was under strict instructions from Iuu not to tell, and she obeyed Iuu.

As to Bungkert, I'm not sure, but I'm inclined to believe that he was also lying, covering for his daughter to leave me completely in the dark.

Bungkert busied himself calling Iuu's cousins and friends, but no one knew of Iuu's whereabouts or merely said so. We drove to Tang's brother Lod in Bandung to find out if he had Kay's telephone number and talked to his wife, Thein, but they said they didn't know, except that Kay was still working at the old Beer Bar on Soi Bua Khao but they didn't know which bar it was.

On Saturday, Bungkert agreed to go with me to Nonghan and file a missing person report with the police. The officer in charge took him aside into a separate room and talked to him at length. Then, finally, a report was filled out that I was asked to sign, and we went back to Nonglard. I stopped at the Bangkok Bank branch and transferred five thousand baht to Iuu's bank account hoping that she would check her balance from time to time and withdraw the funds to keep afloat.

The next day went by and no one arrived from Bangkok. Was there still hope that Iuu might come?

Finally, on Sunday, the folks were gathering outside Rin's house waiting for a pickup truck to arrive, and when it did, Rin and Tao were in it, but not Iuu.

My heart had told me all along that she was in Pattaya. That is where we had met, where she had many friends, including cousin Kay. Iuu was not the type who would venture into unknown territory as I could. She would only go with, or where there was, a cousin or friend. No one other than Geet in Bangkok, the natural destination for her would therefore be Pattaya.

On Monday, April 13, I ended my five-day stay in Nonglard and drove home to Bangkok. I arrived late afternoon, checked our room in the vague hope of finding Iuu, and drove to Geet who said that she was leaving to take the bus home to Chiang Rai. She said Iuu hadn't called, and that she didn't know where Iuu was. Being frustrated in my search but unwilling to give up, I drove to Pattaya checking out the beer bars on Soi Bua Khao and along Beach Road and in Walking Street in South Pattaya.

No sign of Iuu anywhere. I found it hard to look at the girls, shouting their stereo-type "welcome" at me, and as the hours progressed, even blocking my way on the sidewalk trying to grab a hold of me. Turning the corner on Beach Road and Soi Post Office 13/2, a cunt suggested to me, "Big or small, I'll blow you…" I was disgusted and thought to myself, no, Iuu would never go back to this environment. She's not in Pattaya. At around two o'clock at night, I drove back to Bangkok.

Another short and restless night began, night number eight without Iuu, with little eating and no more drinking. I was getting thinner by the day, but also older. If only she would call once, say a couple of words, anything. But nothing. Bungkert had said, "she's fucking with you." Indeed, she was. Whenever we had had some argument before, and she had ran but come back, the punishment she had meted out was always ten times of what I had allegedly done to her. I had told her that and she replied, "I wanted to hurt you."

When she had run off with Kay to introduce her into the Pattaya sex trade, and I protested, Iuu only returned after she had obtained the concession of a new house for mother from me, and then a two-baht (one ounce) gold necklace.

Sometime I felt that I was buying Iuu to be and remain my wife, but then again, for months on end we seemed just a normal couple with no particular demands made by her. The one thing I was beginning to be sure of, though, was that I could never be sure about what the next minutes might bring. Iuu could break out in argument within seconds, unexpectedly, and the air would get thick around us for a few hours or even a day. My sensitivity being reduced by my indulgence in a couple of Singha beers almost every evening didn't help matters much.

"If you love a woman, you have to be smart," said the monk to me later. He was right. If you don't love, you don't hurt, but if you do love, watch out!

I think the same could be said for Iuu. Initially, she said she had married me for my money although not a lot, she said, I had enough while she and her family had nothing. Then she added:

"At first there is no love, but then love comes."

I didn't realize that she was referring to herself, and it makes me happy, even if only in hindsight, that Iuu loved me, and as Geet confirmed to me, Iuu had told her many times. Love that was built over three years of living together as husband and wife, sharing almost every moment, cannot die over night. Mine for Iuu that has become a solid bond cannot, and I believe Iuu's love for me and her bonding is no different.

My experience from a much longer life than Iuu's is, that the hurt that comes with separation of a love relationship can be overridden or pushed aside by a new relationship very easily and quickly, but as soon as that new relationship ends, the former love resurfaces and comes back at an instant because the bond is still intact.

I was once told by a psychologist, that it takes the same number of years to get over a love relationship as the relationship itself had lasted, therefore, in Iuu's and my case, three years until we would be emotionally free of each other. In the meantime, any new relationships that we engage in will be burdened and encumbered making the new partner jealous. Iuu's misguided determination of ending our relationship with brutality is not working, but to the contrary, turns her natural ability to love into a farce and eventually turns away the new partner.

My marriage to Iuu was preceded by nine years of abstinence following a ten-year marriage with two children.

When Iuu and I met, I was really ready for her, and she who had been married for only three months one and a half years earlier, was also free. Marriage by rebound, on the other hand, does not work and usually does not last long.

I checked back with Geet many times whether Iuu had called, and was told each time "no".

"Where is Iuu? Iuu youtinai?"

"Mailoo, mailoo," "I don't know," was Geet's standard answer. I did not believe her. Iuu used to see Geet all the time, or call her. When we were driving about, Iuu's Nokia would ring, Geet calling: "Where are you?" They talked always, and I was certain Geet was merely following Iuu's instructions not to tell me.

One day in Pattaya, I went to the Pattaya Mail newspaper to place an ad, offering a reward of five thousand baht for anyone knowing Iuu's whereabouts. The newspaper hesitated saying they would have to consult with their lawyer as to the infringement of privacy.

I went to a Thai local newspaper and placed an ad by way of an announcement:

"Winner of the ThaiSunset 2004 100,000 baht Cash Beauty Award: อิ๋ว Watcharaporn Schemmann, 22 years old, loving wife of Dr. Michael Schemmann, business owner, university student, and superior chef, of Udon Thani residing in Bangkok" showing Iuu's picture and my telephone number.

I showed the advertisement to Geet and said that I would give Iuu, who loved money, one hundred thousand baht on the spot if she returned.

Then I went to the Pattaya radio station who agreed to air a missing person report for a week.

The radio announcement brought a funny response. While I was walking home from class at ABAC, a lady called talking in Thai with intermittent English words mentioning the words "Iuu", "broken heart", and "rented apartment" on a street whose name I did not understand. I had a Thai friend call her back. The lady effectively said that she was twenty-seven years of age, was from the Northwest of Thailand, came to Pattaya only a few weeks ago, and would be willing to be my girl friend if Iuu did not return. In other words, she had called because she saw an opportunity for herself to garner a farang.

I saw Iuu's teacher at the weekend school that Iuu was attending to get her high school graduation diploma. Iuu had become friendly with the lady teacher, Adjarn Nut, and we had taken her and her husband and daughter out for dinner in Minburi several months earlier and had a very good time together. Adjarn Nut was also from

Udon Thani, and a talkative assertive young women in her late twenties or early thirties. I told Adjarn Nut of the one hundred thousand baht gift for Iuu, and added that I would pay Adjarn Nut ten percent if she were instrumental and successful in returning Iuu home.

Adjarn Nut called me back and said that I should meet her at the Teepveela Wat (Temple) on Ramkhamhaeng Road on a Saturday in late April. I was too excited to ask for details and was hoping that she had been in contact and would show up with Iuu. But she arrived in the company of another teacher, Meaw, and the two began making telephone calls to students some of whom later dropped in and started making calls to their friends. The meeting took all afternoon and part of the evening, but no concrete news or sign of Iuu.

A few days later, a student called me and spoke in broken English that Iuu was living with a girl friend on Ramkhamhaeng Road in Bangkok, not far from our home, and Adjarn Nut had made arrangements to meet Iuu on the weekend at the girl friend's home in Samutpakarn, a city on the ocean just south of Bangkok. I went and bought Iuu a seventeen-thousand-baht one ounce gold bracelet that she had always wanted, together with a new Nokia, and wrote a couple of desperate love lines on a card, and gave it to Adjarn Nut to give to Iuu.

The weekend passed. No news. Nothing. I went to Adjarn Nut's home and found her husband, Sanya, sitting outside the house by a fire drinking whiskey together with a friend. Sanya, said that Adjarn Nut had gone to Udon Thani for ten days after being unsuccessful in meeting Iuu. I asked Sanya where the gift parcel was, and he motioned, saying "inside the house". I eventually persuaded him to give it back to me. He said the mobile phone inside the parcel had rung many times, but he hadn't opened the parcel to answer the calls.

Sanya introduced me to his neighbor, Daeng, a Thai man in his early forties who spoke rather fluent English having studied in Australia. Daeng immediately volunteered to help me to find my wife. For starters, he called Bungkert and told him in clear terms that he knew that Bungkert knew of Iuu's whereabouts and that he better talk. Bungkert refused. An hour later, Bungkert called back and said that he knew.

"Iuu is in Northern Thailand."

All of my foreign colleagues and friends who had noticed Iuu's disappearance told me to sit back and relax.

"She will come back", they all said. "Just give her time."

I found the advice extremely consoling but unhelpful in getting over my agony. Daeng, on the other hand, disagreed completely.

"You have to see Iuu face to face. It is now three weeks, and if you don't find her, she will be gone forever. This is Thailand…"

Love lost is driven by fear more than hope. The morning, Monday, April 26th, I jumped into my car and drove to Nonglard to see Bungkert and hopefully find Iuu there, too.

I've never made the six hundred kilometer journey in less time: six and a half hours.

On arrival, Bungkert and Tang were surprised to see me, and Bungkert immediately admitted:

"I lied to the Thai man. He was pressing me, so I answered I know where Iuu is, but I lied."

Then he said he was afraid of Daeng because he talked so fast, not in Isan, but in Thai. I spent about two hours relaxing, then said good-bye.

"No Iuu, no good."

Bungkert and Tang were as surprised to see me leave, as they were at my arrival. At midnight, I was back in Bangkok, desolate and alone.

On the following Wednesday, Daeng and I went to Geet to have a long talk. Geet said that Iuu was okay but not happy. At the same time, Geet did not say when Iuu had called, or if she had called. Daeng and I knew that Geet was lying.

Geet started talking of all of my mistakes in my marriage, that I had always made big problems out of small ones, that Iuu had selected me, then loved me, and that I had not given her anything back in substance like the house for mother and father when I had paid millions for a franchise, raising doubts in Iuu's mind as to her future. I was shocked to learn how Geet could carry on and on while Iuu had never mentioned anything of the sort but apparently complained to Geet, instead.

Geet said that I must change, but that she and Iuu didn't believe that I could change. As of now I had a fifty percent chance of Iuu returning home.

Daeng and I found Geet's remarks quite revealing and we decided to return to Geet two more times. The next time Geet inquired whether I would be willing to put my promises of a changed marriage into writing, to which I agreed. These were basically the complete equality between Iuu and myself in matters of money, decisions about anything and everything, mutual respect and my undertaking to make Iuu as happy as she had always tried to make me happy. My hopes began to rise.

At the following meeting, Geet said that Iuu would call me direct on or before Sunday, May 2nd, and so she did.

I had just driven Daeng home after another meeting with Geet, when I answered my mobile and had to stop the car to understand the caller. It was a very high pitch voice talking about Iuu.

"What is your name," I asked.

"Iuu," she answered.

"I don't recognize your voice. Are you sure you are Iuu?" I asked back.

"Come on, Michael. I am Iuu." Now I recognized her by her tone and anger. Then Iuu gave me the news that I wrote down so as not to forget:

"I think we don't belong together. I always came back and you put me down again. My family is stupid. I'm no good for you. All men are like this. I don't want anything from you. I want divorce. You don't to the Amphur? I will go to the Amphur and ask." Then she hung up. I had interrupted and said, no I don't want divorce, that I loved her too much, and that I had changed. And I said that she was angry.

Ten minutes later, when I was back home, she called again:

"Okay, I'm angry only five minutes. You know that. Bring everything… (I didn't understand the name of the place), my passport, books, everything." She said it in an angry and demanding tone. "I'm too far away. You cannot find me. No, I don't want to see you again. Finished. I don't love you anymore. Too late. No, I don't wait." Then she hung up again.

In my response to Iuu's barrage of accusations, I had answered:

"Your family is fine. I just spent five days over Songkran with father, mother and brother Tiu. I really love you. Now I fight for you. I will find you and see you face to face. We belong together. I really, really miss you. I will not divorce you. I cannot finish. I always care for you. I know I was wrong. Geet told me."

I was elated to hear her voice, never mind what she had said. Just to have talked to her made my day. At the same time I was devastated about the news, but I also knew inside that this was not Iuu talking, this was an angry woman who for some reason could not find a way out by amiable discussions but by confrontation in absentia.

When times get tough, a mechanism kicks in within me that denies the facts and is determined to change them. It has worked in the past and I believed would work again because beyond the hope, which this determination to fight provides, there is no hope. Nothing is ever final until the fat lady sings, I thought.

The search for "Iuu" went into higher gear. I had made a missing person report both at Pattaya and at Bangkok Hua Mak police stations. The report to the Bangkok police became somewhat uneasy when, after signing the report, I was not dismissed but lead to the investigations section, though not in handcuffs.

The investigator in plain clothes after listening to the details put it to me:

"You killed her."

"No," was my plain and simple answer.

"You killed her because in law, one year from now, you can marry someone of your own kind, a lady professor."

"No, I did not, and I don't want to remarry. I love my wife."

These kinds of question are routine in police investigations, I knew from the movies. Then the officer asked me whether Iuu was a lesbian and liked women. I declined. I gave him the name and telephone number of Geet and asked him to talk to her because I believed that Geet knew of Iuu's whereabouts.

Two weeks later, I went back to the Hua Mak police, found the same investigator, Mr. Sompon, and told him that I had checked with the bank and learned that Iuu had withdrawn five thousand baht from an ATM at Carrefour in Pattaya on Sunday, April 12th, that I had deposited at Nonghan the day before, so was most likely in Pattaya.

After I learned about Iuu's withdrawal, I transferred ten thousand baht into her account, and a week later another ten thousand baht, a total of twenty-five thousand baht since she had left.

"Too much money," said Daeng. "She won't come back until the money runs out. No place to go. But if you keep sending her money, she won't come back."

"I don't want my wife to go fucking in Pattaya only because she has no money," I replied. That was exactly my motive, apart from showing Iuu that I deeply cared for her, which I did.

Daeng and I went to Pattaya to distribute flyers with Iuu's color photo inquiring of her whereabouts and promising a reward of five thousand baht. I drove the car, while he hopped out at Seven-Eleven convenience stores, motorcycle taxi stands, beer bars and hotels, and one hospital, all in South Pattaya along Walking Street, Pattaya Number One and Number Two Roads.

We thought we were successful. Iuu had been shopping at a Seven-Eleven alone buying some dried food, as she did with me, on Number Two Road just two days earlier. A lady on Soi Post Office 13/2 recognized Iuu and said that she saw her on Soi 17 north of North Road (Pattaya Nua). Going there we learned that Iuu had been driven by a motorcycle taxi driver number six to the bus terminal early Wednesday on April 28th, but the taxi driver had meanwhile returned to Udon Thani, but they had his phone number. A call to the driver confirmed that he had driven Iuu to the bus station. She had said that she was going to Bangkok. The driver confirmed her green traveling bag and gray back pack. The motorcycle taxi people, as well as the lady in Soi Post Office, confirmed that Iuu usually left her room at around two o'clock in the afternoon, went to the beach, and returned alone around nine to ten o'clock in the evening.

I was glad to hear that Iuu apparently was not working the beer bar scene, was not in the company of a new farang, and was simply using her time to be alone and reflect. My worry was, the more she was alone, thinking alone, she would only get more angry and paranoid highlighting everything in her mind that did not go her way, rather than getting it out of her chest and becoming normal again.

With Daeng's help, we traced Iuu's call on May 2nd to a mobile phone service near Sathorn Road in Bangkok, confirming the motor cycle driver's statement that she had gone to Bangkok four days earlier. A mosaic began to form tracing her movements, but we were always days behind and unable to meet her.

"You have to meet her face to face to explain," Daeng kept insisting. "Otherwise, in Thailand, she'll be gone. You must think Thai, not farang."

We went back to Geet and learned that Iuu was willing to see me one more time to sign the consensual divorce papers.

"Accept and go," said Daeng, "but don't sign but explain. Only to see her, otherwise you won't see her again."

"I cannot lie to Iuu. If I do, she will be so angry that she will never ever want to see me again," I replied.

"You think farang. That's wrong. You must think Thai."

Iuu's informal education at Teepveela was to start on Sunday, May 10th. Adjarn Nut said that she had not registered, so I went together with Daeng to register for her, pay the tuition of a few thousand bahts and buy the school books. We ran into the head master, Mrs. Onurad who was hostile at first but then became rather friendly asking that I make the donation of a desk and chair, or a cabinet, which I did a few days later, buying a big new desk and office chair for her and delivering it in person.

Iuu had already registered herself during the first week of May, indicating once again that she had left Pattaya for Bangkok. I was relieved and proud of Iuu for continuing the course and getting her high school diploma.

Returning to Geet, we were told that Iuu would be calling me in person before Sunday, May 16th to talk to me, but nothing was said that she was willing to meet with me face to face. Daeng and I were checking out desks at a dealer on Seri Tai Road when my mobile phone rang and Iuu was on the line. It was a much more relaxed call than the first one two weeks before, and though still speaking with an agitated high voice, she did not hang up until ten minutes of conversation. She repeated the old accusations, I rebutted them, she said she wanted a divorce, I replied that would be so difficult for me because I loved her, and without a meeting face to face to discuss, I wouldn't do it. Once again I felt happy and sad both at the same time.

During our conversation, Iuu resorted to a diversion, a plain and straight lie. She said:

"I am now leading the simple life of my people. Very small but happy."

On Monday, Daeng and I went to Pattaya again to check around and look for Iuu because we had traced Iuu's call to a public pay phone at Tesco Lotus on Sukhumvit Road. We distributed some flyers and learned that the motor cycle taxi gang had driven her back to town the other day, but the motor cycle driver was from another "win" using red jackets, freelancing, and they didn't know his name or where he usually worked. Daeng and I drove all over town distributing flyers to all motorcycle wins in red. I had made four hundred flyers, and we had already distributed about three hundred.

We spent several hours at Tesco Lotus hoping that Iuu might return. Then I bought a new TV for father and mother, and on Tuesday, May 18th, Daeng and I drove to Nonglard to meet father and mother to boost morale in Nonglard in my favor. My thinking was that Iuu's final decision of whether to return to our home might depend on mother's, father's, and grandmother's advice. The family is normally consulted in Thailand on very important decision including marriage, education, and house construction.

With Daeng being the interpreter, I did have a meaningful in-depth conversation with mother, and when father came in and took over, as was his nature, with him. After three years, this was the first true face to face interchange I had had with Bungkert, and it was both devastating, revealing, but also bringing hope.

Bungkert basically repeated the allegations I had heard through Geet, and said that any other woman except Iuu would have long left me. There was no mention of his own failings vis-à-vis Tang and the family, and I did not bring them up.

The new TV I had bought for them was not needed, as they already had a large 25-inch TV in place. On question, Taeng said they had paid cash for it. Bungkert changed the story and said the bank had financed it. He declined my offer to volunteer and pay off the bank by saying, "No need. We have one year. The bank wants the interest, not the money now."

Bungkert listened well to my changes in my life, that I had stopped drinking beer on a daily basis, in fact stopped entirely, made believable by my loss of weight down from ninety-four to eighty kilos. He was especially interested in my money situation which now boasted close to a million baht in cash plus more coming from life savings in Switzerland. It would be both Iuu's and my money, and we would consult each other from now on how and where to invest, and that a new home for them for three hundred thousand baht would be okay with me. Also, that I would buy Bungkert the two buffalos that he wanted a few months ago, but I hadn't bought because the price was thirty thousand not ten thousand as Iuu had suggested.

In response to my question why Iuu was leading the small life, Bungkert replied:

"She works in a factory because you gave her only two thousand baht," he said in an accusing voice.

"But Bungkert," I replied, "I put twenty-five thousand baht into her bank account and she knows that. But where in the factory is she working?"

"She is working in production for one hundred seventy baht a day," Bungkert replied.

My respect but also sadness for Iuu rose again. First, she was enrolled in school, finishing with her high school diploma in only eight months. Now she was also foregoing any comforts that we had enjoyed over the past three years by sacrificing herself at minimum wage, basically none, just to be independent and prove to me that she didn't need anyone but was self-sufficient.

Eventually, Bungkert came up with the idea that he and Tang were against divorce, that nothing of substance had happened to warrant it, that Iuu on father's and mother's orders would come to Nonglard so that she and I could meet face to face and clear up anything of the past in order to live together again. The only thing Bungkert could not say was "when", but "sure" "sure" "sure one hundred percent, Iuu will come". He would call Daeng and me, and then we would have to come very quickly, instantly.

Daeng and I returned to Bangkok with the feeling of accomplishment that Iuu and the good times would be back again, at last.

I reflected over Bungkert's claim for a day, then drove to Ban Pakong where Rin, her husband, Gen, and other cousins were working in a sea food packing plant, reasoning that Iuu would never apply anywhere alone, nor would she be accepted unless she was a member of the clan already working there. Iuu had also suggested to her mother, Tang, to flee her husband, Bungkert's abuses by going into hiding in Ban Pakong until Bungkert disappeared having no one to care for him.

I arrived at the factory at seven o'clock in the morning. It was raining, and the umbrella, peaking out from underneath it, somewhat hid me from appearance. A good hundred young and some older women dismounted from buses, pickups, and motorcycles, but Iuu was not among them.

The following day I checked out the village and its apartments, and on further reflection decided that Iuu did not take the huge step back into her Isan tradition to work in a fish factory at five or six thousand baht a month, which was far less than I had given her in pocket money alone every week, only to prove independence. My heart kept telling me that Iuu was in Pattaya and nowhere else.

Once again, on Wednesday, May 26th, I drove to Pattaya and checked around and eventually stopped at a print shop asking for the cost of printing a few thousand of my fliers for a wider distribution than Daeng and I had been able to accomplish. I thought of spreading the flyers to all of the shops, hotels, and anywhere possible. The printer said he had people, but then added why not insert the flyer in the widely read newspapers, the Thairat. He phoned for the price of insertion and circulation and then went ahead making the printing plates while I drove to the two distributors to get the exact circulation and insertion price. The proofs were ready at noon, the number to print was twelve thousand, and at five o'clock the whole lot was delivered to the distributors for the morning and evening delivery in Pattaya, and nearby areas of Chachoengsao and Sattahip.

I drove back to Bangkok and got Daeng to agree to be ready for pick-up at seven in the morning so that we could receive the calls on the way to Pattaya and get there by nine o'clock to look up Iuu, because any minute later would cause Iuu, who would hear about the campaign, to flee and we would have missed her. The flyers showed Iuu's beautiful face in color, a quite distinct face that stands out and is easily remembered, with the words "Missing Person. 5,000 baht Reward. Iuu Watcharaporn Schemmann. Call Daeng… Telephone Number."

By the time we arrived in Pattaya on this Thursday, May 27th, at around nine o'clock in the morning, Daeng had answered five or more calls with hot tips. We drove to the first informer and were given a place where Iuu went daily in the company of a blond farang in his mid to late thirties.

My heart sank, but rose again on the prospect of seeing Iuu. We drove quickly to the Soi between Pattaya Tai and Pattaya Klang on the south side of Sukhumvit, and while I waited at the intersection, Daeng went into the alley on foot to the exact house number to make his observations and report back to me. Instead of going with him, I waited in the car, but after a few minutes of hesitation got out and walked down the alley when Daeng waived at me to come quickly.

An older and two younger women had been sitting in the yard, he said, one sleeping in an arm chair, the other crouching down on the ground eating. As I arrived, the older woman had already spotted me and no one was there.

I simply opened the gate and went inside. The old woman blocked the door to the house, and a man appeared. Daeng began explaining that we were looking for Iuu.

"No Iuu here," replied the old woman.

Daeng talked some more, like he had seen two of them, etc.

"Kai, Kai, come out," the woman banged against the door of a room.

Iuu's cousin Kai appeared and spun around the moment she saw me, going back to the room, closing the door.

Iuu was inside with her. I had missed her.

Parked outside was a brand new, red Honda Wave 100 motorcycle without a license plate. It was Iuu's.

We received another phone call a few hours later from Iuu's real landlord. She said that Iuu had just checked out and we could come and talk. Upon arrival, the lady demanded identification from me, and when I showed her our marriage certificate changed her attitude instantly and became friendly, trying to help.

We talked for a good hour and saw Iuu's apartment that she had just vacated in a hurry; the checkout which Iuu did not attend but her Thai family did, arriving with a truck, leaving behind a huge fifty-inch color TV.

Iuu had moved into the apartment about six weeks ago together with a blond, blue-eyed Swedish man of about thirty-five years of age who paid the monthly rent of 13,000 baht, had bought Iuu a thick five baht gold necklace, and an equally weighty gold bracelet (altogether five ounces of gold), a new motorcycle and the big color TV. Iuu had said they were building a home at Soi Nern Pabwan that would be ready soon.

Iuu was a big spender, the lady said, was carrying large bills in her pocket, but always taking away the tips that her boyfriend left after paying for meals or at the bar.

"I remember," I said, "that's Iuu from Isan, you know."

"Iuu always bosses the man around and tells him everything, and then he does," said the land lady. "She is always in a bad mood, drinks a lot of Heineken beer and smokes."

"Is she fat?" I asked.

"Yes, quite fat." I knew Iuu loves to eat.

"Iuu, again," I said. "She was quite chubby when she left. Actually I liked her that way."

"In what language did they talk," I asked.

"English," said the landlady, "but they didn't talk much. Just sat there, and if the man wanted to talk to anyone else, Iuu quickly prevented it. He is not going to live very long. He looks really sick in the face."

"Why," I asked.

"Drugs, I think," said the lady. "He's on some drugs. They want to open a beer bar in Pattaya. When the money is gone, Iuu will tell him bye-bye."

"I can't wait," I replied laughing, "I want my wife back."

"You are a handsome man," the lady egged me on, "but I know, love makes blind" and she added in German: "Liebe macht blind."

The lady's husband of sixteen years was a German and she had been living and working with him in Hamburg. Her German was far better than her English and I did not need Daeng's interpretations to converse with her.

Then the lady mentioned some facts that were a shock to me:

"Iuu was introduced to me by her mother who had been working for me and my husband's beer bar about twenty years ago. She said to me a couple weeks ago, this is Iuu. Remember my daughter?"

"What do you mean," I said with consternation. "Are you saying Iuu's mother Tang is here now?"

"Yes," she replied, and her family.

"Are you saying, Tang was working for you as a bar girl twenty years ago?"

"Yes, of course, she did. I had many girls from Isan."

"And what about Iuu?" I insisted.

"Iuu was about four years old and living here too. Tang had brought her with her from Isan."

"And how long did she work for you?" I inquired further.

"Oh, for about three to four years."

"Was she taking men home, too?" I asked.

"Well, you know the beer bar business. They all do," she replied with a smirk on her face.

I thought of Iuu's brother, Tiu. I knew Bungkert was working in Saudi Arabia and Libya for nine years since Iuu's birth and came home only once as Iuu remembered. To remember dad come home, Iuu must have been around four to five years old when Tiu was already born. Thinking of Tiu, he looks a lot like his mother, but Bungkert's features that Iuu has, Tiu does not have at all. But then again, Tiu's features are not Lukueng, the mix of farang and Thai or Isan. I don't know what to make of the story, so I dismissed it in it's entirety. Perhaps the landlady was hoping to enrage me, but I wasn't so that the matter was dropped.

I did know, however, that particularly Isan mother's who had worked in Pattaya in their youth were encouraging their daughters to do likewise, and even getting brutal over it as did Thein with her daughter Kai who eventually obliged and now seems to like the easy lifestyle.

In the late afternoon we followed up another caller's tip and found Iuu's new house on Soi Nern Pabwan, just about a kilometer east of Sukhumwit Soi 53. It was about a week away from completion and had cost 2.7 million baht or $70,000. We learned from the registry office that it was registered in the name of Tang-On, Iuu's mother's name. Iuu could not have it registered in her own name without me signing as well, and signing away any claim, thus her paranoia about our divorce.

About a week later, I was in Pattaya again, and my car drove into Soi Nern Pabwan as if on impulse, then into Iuu's village past the bridge over the railroad tracks, and stopped in front of her house. As I got out, I heard a scream. The gate and the house door were open. A stooped blond, blue-eyed man in his mid-thirties was sitting on the balcony looking at me as I walked passed him, with my camera in hand taking a quick picture. I kept on walking right into the furnished living room, glanced around in a flash for Iuu and then ran upstairs. There were four doors, and not knowing which one to open I stopped as Kai came running up behind me screaming:

"Get down there, get down there."

I took a picture of her, as well, and descended the stairs.

Mother Tang was sitting on the sofa, next to Iuu's brother, Tiu, completely still and complacent not knowing what to make of the situation. I kept on walking and once outside the man stopped me and asked why I had taken his picture.

"Follow me onto the road, " I replied, "I'll talk to you." I motioned several times, then he followed me.

"I am Iuu's husband. What is your name?"

"I am Balliard" or something, he replied in what I thought sounded like a Scottish accent. He was in early forties, I thought, had some bond hair, empty blue eyes and a bland ashen face.

He said he lived with Kai who was chubby and could not attract anyone better. But this was a straight lie as I learned two months later. He actually was Iuu's new farang.

Not knowing who he was, I said that I meant no trouble but that I was deeply hurt by Iuu's running away in only five minutes and going into hiding over a non-event. He listened, trembling slightly and obviously afraid.

"Why did you take my picture," he wanted to know.

"I always take pictures," I replied. "And here's my card. No, I give you two. Tell your Swedish friend to give me a call. Call me yourself anytime you wish."

Then I went back to my car and backed out of the narrow street. I would have liked to say to Balliard:

"You bastard are fucking and paying Kai while her husband is waiting in Isan wanting her back, and her six-year old son Wai doesn't have a mother. Did she ever tell you, or don't you care?"

I was driving back into Pattaya when the mobile phone rang. It was Iuu:

"Fuck you," where her first words.

Then she said she was happy which I said I knew she wasn't. She said the new man was nice to her. I said he was a sick druggy who wouldn't live long.

"Up to him what he does," she replied without denying it.

She reiterated that she wouldn't come back to me. I replied that our home is waiting and that I loved and cared for here deeply.

"I want to meet you face to face," I insisted.

"What for"? she snapped back.

"Because how you left was not nice. We always said if we part we do it nicely not like this."

"I'm talking to you. That's nice," she replied.

"No it isn't. But then you could call me sometime like once every two weeks or so," I suggested.

"What for?" she quipped, "I finished you."

"That's what you think," I answered, "it takes two to finish, but you only ran."

She hung up.

Two minutes later she called again.

"I am happy now. I was never happy with you."

"Come on, Iuu, we were happy so many times. Now you are lying," I suggested in a mild but determined voice.

"I will not come back to you. Please let me go," she wined.

"We can talk about that. Tell me when and where I can see you."

"No," was her brutal but simple response. Then she hung up.

Once again, I was happy, if only to now know the facts of her whereabouts, because the greatest agony comes from not knowing.

I checked the bank again and learned that the next twenty thousand baht I had sent had been withdrawn from Udon Thani on May 1st and May 2nd, and had obviously been used to pay for Bungkert's and Taeng's new 25-inch color TV. I doubt that Iuu had ever used the money, but believe had simply sent the bank book together with her ATM card and the pin number to her mother to make use of the money as she pleased.

I had objected many times of being treated like another ATM machine. I need not complain anymore. Iuu and her family have found a brand new one from Sweden, at least until the money runs out.

It is not my intention to spoil Iuu's business of getting a hold of another man's wealth to put into her and her family's own pockets. Let us remember that Thai marriages, or at least Isan ones, are not based on the notion of romance and love forever until death does us part, but economic survival, sex being merely part of the contract.

Thinking about Iuu's business venture in this way still leaves the door open for her return, because what she does with the Swede is exactly what she did with her first Isan husband of three months from the neighboring village of Banchiang, and her mother was part of the pillage each time. They didn't do it to me, or I didn't let them, whatever, so I have no ax to grind.

If Iuu had any class, she could have phoned and told me: "Look I ran into this Swedish farang while I was contemplating our marriage, and now what do I do, say no? It was you who started all this, remember?"

I could have answered:

"Okay, I'm not the first one and the last you are fucking, and you are not the first for me either, but I love you. When do you think you are finished with the guy?"

She could have answered: "When his money runs out or he gets more sick or dies, may be a year or so. Then I have a nice house for us in Pattaya. Meanwhile enjoy yourself. I'll come and see you from time to time."

This is how Thai husbands are dealt with. What makes me different?

On June 4, 2004, I received a letter from a lawyer in Pattaya and rushed to Daeng to have it translated:

> "Dear Michael Schemmann
> Matter re Divorce
> Michael and Watcharaporn made marriage together since 2544. So, Watcharaporn has big problem, cannot stay together. Now Watcharaporn doesn't want to stay with Michael. I, on behalf of Watcharaporn as lawyer, will let you know to contact me for talking about divorce within seven days. If you have question, contact me at my office above. Please you give good cooperation.
> Sincerely,
> Amnat"

I didn't hesitate to reply:

> "Dear Sir:
> Re: 53/2547
> I have your letter dated 31 (the month I cannot read) 2547. I believe you are confused. I love my wife, Watcharaporn, with all my heart, adore her, respect her, and support her in all matters required and much more.
> My wife loves me back. I attach a print-out of her e-mail to me dated April 4, 2004.
> Sincerely,
> Dr. Michael Schemmann"

The email "Iuu" had sent me only days before she ran, read:

"Dear Dr.Michael . How are you today? I'm not so good. You know why? Because I miss you so much. Please send email to me. LOVE. Mrs.Schemmann "

I believe, Iuu's email spoke the truth, and my response to her lawyer spoke the truth. So far, I haven't heard back from them. I checked with a lawyer and learned that Iuu must wait three years before she can apply for divorce based on separation. I must wait one year before I can apply for divorce based on abandonment. The cop at Bangkok Hua Mak was right but for the wrong reasons.

I do not intend to appease Iuu in her request for divorce because I love her, and love her deeply, in a love that forgives, that hopes, and that is certain of a reunification.

In the meantime I just might heed Iuu's unspoken advice that she should have offered if she had any class. Iuu is normally big hearted but petty minded now. What can I expect, I hadn't raised her to class during the three years I could have. I always showed myself as a conservative unwitting idiot, an ugly old man, as she complained from time to time when she was angry because I was afraid she might return to the Pattaya beer bar scene and fuck again.

Female beauty and youth, if one looks for it, abounds in Pattaya, new merchandise arriving by the bus-loads almost daily. The only trouble Iuu gave me who at one time was one of them, was that I fell in love with her very deeply that turned into suffering when she left.

There are thousands of eighteen to twenty-one year olds, all too often from "Udon" the province, or "Udon Thani" if they are from the city, with pretty though not always beautiful faces, engaging smiles, firm breasts and pink cunts, who, for only fifteen hundred baht, will make pleasant conversation in acceptable English while they bathe you in a Jacuzzi, rubbing their excitement against yours and all over your body, and finally offer themselves and their sex in any way and position your fantasy and treasure desires, then, after an hour or two, say a sweet good-bye and "until next time", without any demands on your pocket book as does the mother and her family back home in Isan, and the father who does likewise but at your expense, all in return for renting their daughter whom you had fallen in love with and possibly married.

Back home in Isan they must think you are stupid, and therefore need not show any responsibility. Indeed, under such circumstances, they are right. You are stupid. There is no law against, and nothing wrong anywhere in the world for, exploiting the stupid, because they are asking for it.

What happened to us, Iuu and me, may be useful for having Iuu for a long time, because the path on which we were going was not healthy and enduring. I worked too much, and she didn't have anything to do. I took her for granted while she had higher aspirations. We needed shock treatment and received it. Would I have been able to provide what Iuu is taking from the new farang? Yes, I have a business of my own that is flourishing aside from teaching at the university. Would I have parted with my funds to put Iuu's share into her pockets? Yes, I was bent on it as she matured. Would I have provided for father and mother the way the new farang is doing now? No. They would have received their survival portion and nothing extra. Would that have disgraced Iuu? No, so long as she could show her own achievements to her villagers.

So, why was all this heartache necessary? It wasn't, but it happened. This is Thailand. Farangs are ill-prepared for this sweet, seductive and at the same time brutal world, and I was one of them, but no longer.

The real victim in all this suffering and striving for material wealth is not me, it is Iuu. She spends her best years in the arms of either sick or older men, but not in the joy and excitement of her own, her own culture, her own games and fun, let alone her age because age in Thailand doesn't seem to matter, but spends her life with these despicably different farang only because she and her mother cannot wait. Eventually, we, the farang, are always finished, but then what?

Why, I have been asked many times by Thai colleagues, why I spend my life with a young and poor Isan woman, feeding her family, rather than a Thai of somewhat equal status. My own brother, visiting from Australia, asked me that question. I never replied. If I wanted to reply, I would say this:

Yes, the people of Isan are not the true Thais who come from Bangkok Province. Yes, they are poor because they don't want to learn. Learning for them is painful because they are drop outs, leaving school at the age of twelve to work on the farm, and to get back into the rhythm of learning is exhausting and "no fun." So they try to overcome their disadvantage by marrying well.

Marrying farang normally solves their material problems at once. In Isan, they don't care about the stigma carried by Thai women marrying a foreigner. Being "mia ferang" is a status Isan women enjoy and carry with pride. By marrying farang, Isan women contribute forty billion baht in foreign currency to the country annually, or about six percent of the regions gross domestic product, by their "life styles" (The Nation, Bangkok, June 14, 2004, page). I am one of them, and Iuu reported with pride a little while ago that the province of Udon Thani, her home, had the highest percentage of farang-to-local marriages.

Thai is bland, Isan is rich. Rich emotionally, rich physically because they are of strong build, their flesh, muscles and spirits are strong and receptive to the touch, and rich because they have problems I can help alleviate and even solve if only I have the patience. Isan needs, me, Thai doesn't. Being not needed is like not existing.

"Any Thai man would have walked away and left Iuu alone," I've been advised.

"Take another one," said Mrs. Long of Sureena Hotel in Pattaya who, three years ago, had once advised me: "Take an eighteen year-old."

I, a farang raised in the tradition of Parcival and the Niebelungen Sagas with its Troubadourian romance and truth, cannot abandon a love object, but must fight to fulfill myself. I can do this only by mixing my emotions with Thai values of sanook for fun for fun's sake, and not falling in love again so easily, while waiting for my true love object to sort herself out and return. If she doesn't, the sanook simply continues and we miss each other for the rest of our lives.

There is something about Thailand: It sucked me in, as I read that Thailand became a home of choice to many for perhaps the same reasons. I don't know.

When I arrived the first time as a tourist for ten days, twenty years ago, it was all fun and amazement.

The second time I arrived, Thailand changed my life in a hurry. I had a job and purpose, and fell in love, was accepted and married. Iuu showed me her country and explained. While I was struggling, she supported and loved me for what reason I didn't care in the least because I needed her.

Now, three years later, being told by Iuu that we have failed, which I don't believe, I cannot simply return to my home abroad. I look at my own kind, these farang women at the beaches and am turned off. I see my previously favorite movie stars on screen, like Julia Roberts in "The Mexican", or even Grace Kelly in "High Noon", the oldie, and they don't turn me on anymore. My taste buds for farang food changed along with the preferences for facial and sexual features: the fine chiseled faces of Southeast Asian women. Their seductive and submissive smiles however deceitful, I know, if they are out to procure; their almond eyes and slightly tanned skin with the touch of silk.

I remember the strictures of my Western culture, its anal retentiveness about being proper and adapted, and I just don't care for it anymore. And I don't care anymore about what Westerners call for progress, security and wealth because it comes at the ruin of emotional freedom, personality, and togetherness.

In Thailand I am surrounded by masses of people in crowded streets, cities, markets and malls, universities, beaches. Wherever I go, space is confined but also comforting because it is filled with Thais. I am never alone.

Is Thailand clean? No. Is Thailand fair and just? No. Is Thailand happy? Yes. Is Thailand welcoming us farang? Yes and no, but mostly yes.

Iuu is a victim, too, by adopting a part of my romance and falling in love with me. Her denial now by resorting to brutality is proof, because if she was not in love she would be indifferent and agree to meet and talk. She will not convince her heart and soul but merely inflict needless suffering to gain space.

Iuu is not one hundred percent Isan anymore, but Mia farang. We have lived together for most of her formative years while the pretty teenager she was at nineteen turned into a beautiful and seductive woman of twenty-three who is well aware of her armor, knows Western culture, has a high school education, seen the world and speaks what in Thailand goes for perfect English.

I have written this book so that she can read, because she doesn't allow me to see and talk to her; or people who read in her village can tell her, therefore the Thai translation. I want Iuu my wife back, and I don't want to wait thirty years until she is in her fifties and has me cremated because we never divorced, saying to herself: "Father and mother are dead now, too. I have no daughter to send to Pattaya. Of all the men I had, to get me all this wealth that I don't really need, maybe Michael was my true husband. Maybe I should have listened, seen and talked to him. He was my first farang. He really loved me."

Chapter 16
Epilogue

An epilogue, or after word, as opposed to a prologue, a foreword, is a short passage added at the end of a book, telling about a future event or conclusion.

By June 2004, having struck gold for two months now by catching the Swedish farang, "Iuu's" ferocious and unbridled appetite, and her heavy beer intake, had gained her as much weight as I had lost during the agony of searching for her. Iuu now weighed-in a hefty sixty kilograms, her tummy was bulging and her clothes bursting at the seams. She looked at least like twenty-eight, a good five or six years over her true age. Also, one pack of Marlboro Lights rarely lasted one day.

Iuu never liked physical exercise, walking, let alone swimming. She would rather sit on the motorbike even to go a few houses away. She rationalized that her Buddha Prah was the reclining one, and given her blood type zero she was predestined by nature to sit more than stand or walk.

Several months after I had surprised Iuu in her new house on Soi Nerd Plabwan in Pattaya, while alone in the kitchen preparing dinner, she had a very sudden and intense head ache, began feeling dizzy, then collapsed, slumped to the ground and was gasping for air.

Mother Tang, brother Tiu and farang Swede were watching a Thai show in the living room, the TV blaring, no one noticed what was going on in the kitchen until farang Swede, in need of a new Heineken, went to the fridge and saw Iuu stretched out on the floor.

The man had been a hush puppy all his life, was startled and ran back into the living room motioning Tang to come and see for herself. Tiu did not even move.

By the time Tang finally understood, being slow in whatever she did, Iuu was unconscious and lifeless. Tang knelt down over Iuu, turning her on her back and talking to her intensely without any reaction or result. Then she fumbled for the cure-all menthol stick and poked it into Iuu's nostrils, but there was hardly any air going in or coming out.

Farang Swede had grabbed the Nokia and was asking Tang frantically in English: "What is the Thai number for nine-one-one?"

Neither Tang nor Tiu, who had meanwhile joined the trio in the kitchen, had any idea what the Swede was yelling about. They merely stared at him in their catatonic stupor.

Then mother with Swede's help began to drag Iuu back into the upright position, but to no avail. She slumped right back and hit her head hard on the marble kitchen floor.

Farang Swede decided: "This is too much," ran out the front door, started the motorcycle and took off for the nearest Scandinavian bar ordering a few Heineken for himself, a pack of smokes, and the Swedish newspaper which they carried especially for him and his friends.

Eventually, neighbors were alerted by the commotion in the house, an ambulance was called arriving a good thirty minutes later after maneuvering through thick and slow rush hour traffic on Sukhumvit Road and Soi Nern Pabwan.

The paramedics took forever, it seemed, to put Iuu on a stretcher and attach the safety belts, strapped an oxygen mask on her face but the oxygen bottle was nearly empty, then started given her a heart massage until mother Tang began to plead with them until they stopped what Tang thought was more a sexual assault.

Iuu had said to me many times:

"I may die here. Whenever your time is up there is nothing you can do."

That she may die young I knew, given her weight, lack of exercise, and boom-boom attitude in going about her life, and I had told her so. Perhaps this was her time. She had achieved everything she had hoped for while still quite young. The new house and furniture were worth a good three million bath, setting mother, in whose name it was, up for the rest of her life.

I remember the day precisely. I had been to Wat Teepveela in the morning, praying for our marriage and making my offerings, then gone home to put the finishing touches on my book when the phone rang. Not the mobile, but the room phone that hadn't rung in ages it seemed.

A somber lady's voice in perfect American English was on the line:

"Can I speak to Dr. Michael, please," she asked rather stiff and formally.

"Speaking," I replied.

"I am calling from Bangkok Pattaya Hospital in Pattaya," she said.

"Yes," I replied, "what can I do for you?"

"Are you the husband of Mrs. Watcharaporn Schemmann? We found your calling card from Assumption University in her belongings."

"Yes, yes, sure, " I stuttered. "Belongings, belongings, what belongings are you referring to?"

Iuu's lawyer's letter blitzed in my mind. Suicide because I had refused divorce? I don't think so, but what in the world had she done? I got frightened of having failed her... again...

"I am informing you that your wife is in the trauma center under emergency care," said the nurse in a stern and unemotional voice. "You may visit anytime, twenty-four hours."

"Has my wife asked for me?" I inquired, concerned that I may run into the farang Swede and that my unwelcome appearance only made matters worse.

"No, your wife is not talking," said the nurse.

"I am leaving right now. I'll be there in about an hour," I replied. "Should I be prepared?"

"Yes, you should be," was her answer.

I grabbed my keys and wallet, was in the elevator in a few seconds, and onto the motorway to Pattaya a few minutes later. It was Sunday evening, the time eight-thirty, a light drizzle was hitting my windshield, but the main traffic was going in the other direction with city folks returning to Bangkok from their outings on the ocean shores.

Doing slightly over a hundred-forty clicks per hour between the northern and southern toll booths, in the prolonged right turn the pickup tried to spin out of control on the slippery pavement but I caught it by a slight adjustment on the steering wheel, the new 15 inch wheels and Michelin tires clutching the pavement. On Highway Number 3, I maneuver around a few slow moving trucks by going onto the parking lane, eventually made Pattaya's Sukhumvit Road, made a U-turn south of Pattaya Nua, pulling into the Bangkok Pattaya Hospital's emergency parking lot shortly before ten o'clock at night.

I had called ahead from the car and asked that a security guard meet and clear me, and show me to Iuu's room. They would do so, the operator had said and so they did.

I cannot describe my emotions as I entered the emergency room. They were barely under control for I hadn't seen Iuu for several months now and hadn't expected to find her under these circumstances at all.

The room was dimly lit, the oxygen machine was pumping quietly and regularly, the fluid bottle hanging on a stand running the tube into her vein, the EKG was giving off its beeps every second, and there she lay, gray-faced and still with her eyes closed, motionless.

The guard left. I was just standing and looking at her beautiful but lifeless features, feeling a big lump in my throat choking me. I went over to her and kissed her ever so lightly, one or two of my tears falling down on her cheek.

"Iuu," I said softly, "Iuu, I know you can hear me. I am Michael, your husband. I love you, I love you, I love you, please wake up, please wake up for me."

There was no response whatsoever, no facial reaction, or a change in her breathing under the machine. Then the nurse came in joined me for a few minutes of silence. Then she said:

"Can I see your I.D., please?"

I reached for my wallet and pulled out a copy of our marriage certificate that I always carried since searching for Iuu. I gave it to her.

"It's fine," she replied, "I will make a copy and give it back to you later, okay"?"

I nodded.

"Before you go home, we will ask you to sign an authorization for emergency treatment to accept responsibility for the costs. Can you do that"?

"Yes, I will do that," I replied. "We have hospital insurance through Assumption University. But I don't intend to go home until I know that Watcharaporn is recovering. Can you roll a bed in so I can be with my wife. I know her hearing may still be working and it is important for her and myself…" I babbled.

"Not a problem, we actually encourage that," replied the nurse and left the room.

"How long will Iuu remain in this condition before she wakes up, you think?" I asked.

"We cannot make any predictions. We do our best. Please understand," was her somber response.

"Have you performed a CAT-scan of her head, yet?" I inquired.

"That is scheduled for seven o'clock in the morning," replied the nurse.

"I am afraid we cannot wait that long," I replied. "If my wife is suffering from an aneurysm, every further treatment will be too late. I would like to speak to the neurosurgeon on call."

"Are you a medical doctor?" asked the nurse in a somewhat accusative voice.

"Yes, I have had extensive medical training. Take it from there."

I didn't dare ask any further questions and the nurse left the emergency room. A few minutes later she returned with the head nurse.

"We have spoken with the neurosurgeon and he is on his way. Since you are a medical doctor and your wife is the patient, he immediately agreed to come to the assistance of a colleague."

A few minutes later, Iuu was placed on a new bed, oxygen mask and tank replaced by a portable one, and wheeled out of the emergency room down the long corridor to the elevator.

In the lobby, I spotted mother Tang and brother Tiu. When they saw me, they looked away, rose and began walking towards the stairwell. The elevator arrived and took us up to the radiation department.

On the way up, I continued my monologue with Iuu:

"Iuu," I said matter-of-factly, "we are bringing you to the Radiation Department to have a CAT scan done on your head, just to make sure everything is okay inside. I love you, darling. You will be all right. Okay?"

Then I choked up again and had to stop talking.

The long procedure of preparing Iuu for the scan began by injecting radiation fluid into her left arm vein while I watched in silence. The hospital staff had provided me with a white facemask, a green surgeon's cap and gown, and offered me latex gloves that I stuck into my pocket.

A nurse arrived with the authorization forms. I signed without reading. Then she asked me for a down payment of seventy-five thousand bath. I handed her my VISA gold card and signed the voucher minutes later.

The time was now half past midnight. Two endless hours had gone by until Iuu was rolled into the big yellow machine and placed into the long round tube, her head first. All the while I was talking to her softly about the weather, how much I liked Pattaya and the ocean, and that I loved her so much that I had come immediately when I got the news of her accident.

"Everything will be alright, Iuu," I consoled her while inside I was totally torn up and choking.

I was offered a chair next to the surgeon watching the monitor, slice by slice as the CAT was scanning Iuu's brain.

"There, there," the surgeon pointed his finger at a rupture. "Look, Dr. Michael, a break in the artery. Here, another one."

"My God," was all I could reply breaking out in a cold sweat. "She has two aneurisms."

The chance of survival if treated immediately was reasonably good, I knew. But with the old techniques used in Thailand, and the slow pace of testing and treatment, they could be lower than fifty-fifty.

"The bleeding has stopped," mentioned the surgeon.

"We don't know when it resumes, though," I replied. "Reduce the fluid intake immediately."

The surgeon motioned a nurse and gave her instructions in Thai. I didn't need to see any more and took a chair at the back of the room.

Iuu was dying unless surgical intervention was performed right away. The scan took another five minutes to complete. Then the surgeon came over to me and sat down for a minute of silence, then said:

"We will keep your wife in the emergency ward for further observation, then we will decide what to do. She may have suffered permanent brain damage already. We have to perform more tests. Now we don't know," he advised.

The hospital was going to let Iuu die a merciful death if she had permanent brain damage, I thought. How do they really know that? No way, Jose!

"I am fully aware of the risk of permanent brain damage," I responded with some force in my voice. "As her husband, I will care for her, no matter what her condition is or will become. Just give me my wife back, Doctor, please."

"Okay," if those are your instructions, your decision. We can operate tomorrow evening. We are booked up for the morning and afternoon," replied the surgeon.

"Too late, my colleague. I ask that you operate at seven in the morning, the earliest time possible. One hundred thousand bath for you in an envelope, my friend," I said and looked him straight in the eyes.

He didn't flinch, then nodded.

"Seven in the morning it is. I have to go home now to get some rest," then he rose and before he left the room I asked:

"What technique do you use, Doctor. Balloon, clip, or the new spiral."

"I have good experience with titanium clips," he replied.

"Thank you. Fine with me," I concurred. "And please attach this little thing to the clip, if you can."

He looked at the two-millimeter thing for a second and confirmed: "I understand." Then the surgeon left.

I spent a restless night in a chair next to Iuu's bed, happy to hear the sound of the EKG ticking away, the fluid into her arm reduced to a trickle to prevent her blood from becoming thin which could cause the bleeding to resume, and if it did, all other treatment might come too late.

I had stopped talking to Iuu to give her rest, because early in the morning at around five o'clock she would be put under deep, very, very deep by the anesthetist. The brain operation could take anywhere from four to seven hours. A hole would have to be drilled to make an opening in her thick Isan skull before the surgeons could enter the brain and plug the bulges in the artery walls by applying clips made of titanium.

Any mishap along the way, and permanent brain damage would result. Yes, they could give me Iuu back, but with seizures and bursts of uncontrollable anger, or as a vegetable.

"Don't think too much," Iuu had said so many times, and I began following her advice, choking up again, a few tears quietly running down my face.

I began to pray.

"Our father who art in heaven… I need your strength and wisdom. Please give me my Iuu back. I will respect, love and care for her no matter what condition she will be in, and what hardships they may cause. Please let my young wife live. Her life as a beautiful woman has only just begun… "

I must have dozed off briefly when a couple of nurses entered the room. The watch showed it was a quarter past five in the morning. The moment of truth had arrived.

I donned the surgical cap and gown and followed the team into the operating room. Two anesthetists were already waiting acknowledging us with a nod of the head. Then I sat next to Iuu and started talking to her:

"You are getting treatment for your headache, Iuu. You will not be able to hear me for a while, now. But I remain here all the time. I won't leave you. Okay. Talk to you later."

As the recisely measured dose of anesthetics was injected into Iuu's left arm vein, her complexion grew even more pale and gray. After two hours, already in a coma, she was also deeply unconscious. Shortly after seven, the surgeon and an assistant arrived. I said that I would retire to the lounge, as my presence was not needed. They agreed and I left. Leave professional matters in the hands of professionals, I said to myself.

I went to the cafeteria downstairs, had a coffee and doughnut, and then stepped outside for a smoke. It was raining lightly. I liked the tropical warm rain that took away the heat. The traffic was already thick on Sukhumvit Road.

We were now married for over three years. "You have me for a long time, " Iuu had always affirmed. I thought so it shall be.

"You must pull through, Iuu," I spoke to myself. "I need you so much. You must keep your promise."

I was choking up again, threw away the cigarette bud and stepped inside taking a rest on a sofa in the lounge.

The hours ticked by and by, patients where wheeled around in wheel chairs, sad to see each other off, and happy in reunion. From time to time I heard the siren of an ambulance. At two o'clock in the afternoon I got nervous, and at three o'clock I felt I should ask a nurse, but quickly abandoned the urge, stepped outside and had another smoke, then returned to the lounge and kept on praying simply repeating the Lord's prayer, and appealing to Lord Buddha. I saw no conflict in observing both religious rites.

Nurses where running around and I was watching them intensely until at four-thirty in the afternoon one was heading in my direction. She had a stern business-like look on her face. I rose as she approached me. I hadn't met her before.

"Dr. Michael?" she asked as she stood in front of me.

"Yes," I replied my voice quivering.

"The operation has been successful," she stated.

"Oh, thank you," I replied completely overwhelmed by the news. "Thank you, thank you."

"You may go home now or take a hotel room. Your wife is in the wakeup room. It will be several hours before the anesthesia begins to wear off. Then you can come back and see her."

Then she left. I sat down covering my head, broke down and wept. I knew Iuu was safe now in the wake-up room. Perhaps in the morning she might wake up and come out of her coma.

I took a room in our hotel on Soi Post Office that we used to frequent on our brief holidays to Pattaya, the Sureena Hotel, and crashed on the bed without taking my clothes off.

When I awoke it was close to midnight. I took a shower, walked outside and strolled along the seashore on Beach Road. The traffic and the whores looking for customers were the same, day after day, year after year. When does this place ever stop, I thought to myself.

An hour later I returned to my room and was back at the hospital at eight o'clock in the morning.

Iuu was already back in the emergency room, her head bandaged up, pale and gray in the face, hooked up to the fluid bottle that was dripping away again, the ruptures in the arties in her brain having been clipped and closed, relieving the pressure from the flow of blood into her head that had put her into a coma.

I was watching her face with compassion and sorrow, softly massaging her arms and legs from time to time, when, all of a sudden, I felt a reaction in her arm. I called the nurse and told her about it.

Then a doctor came in and reassured himself that Iuu was coming back. It was the happiest moment I had experienced for a very long time. My wife was going to live. Iuu was coming back into our lives!

First her right arm, then her left, were beginning to move about, first slowly than energetically striking out while her eyes remained closed. The nurses came and tied her strong arms to the railing so she could not hurt herself.

From time to time Iuu groaned and moaned calling out indiscernible but beautiful words. The morning went by and I saw that she was thirsty but she could not have any water for fear of vomiting. I got the nurse to bring me a bucket of ice cubes and rubbed them against her lips. She started sucking up the moisture eagerly and I gave her more, little by little.

It was already getting dark outside. At about five in the afternoon, having moved her arms about for hours, and strong arms she had, I recognized that one of Iuu's eyes was slowly opening, then the other one, and by eight o'clock she was looking around full face and saw me.

"Hello, Iuu," I said.

She didn't respond and closed her eyes, then opened them again and looked at me.

"You are in the hospital, Iuu," I said. "You are going to be fine..." She tried to smile but it became only a frown.

I was happy, so happy, I cannot even tell, and continued to hold Iuu's hand, squeezing it from time to time. Then she began squeezing me back.

Iuu was kept in the hospital for another week. I visited every day all day long. When mother Tang and Tiu showed up, I discretely left the room.

A week later, the team of doctors decided to discharge Iuu to recover at home. I had no idea what her intentions were, where home was going to be, and I hadn't asked her. Being so happy that she had made it was perfectly good enough for me.

We had been walking in the corridor the last few days, and she could leave the hospital on her own strength.

I had brought her new clothes that I had bought at the Royal Garden Mall, and she put them on while I was waiting outside in the corridor. When she was finished, she came out towards me, tiptoed and kissed me, whispering into my ear:

"You know I love you very much. Now let's go home. Where is the car?"

"In the parking lot," I replied.

I kissed her back and hugged her for a good minute, I guess. Then I helped her into the stroller, wheeled her out to the parking lot and drove us home to ABAC.

The university gave me the rest of the term off so that I could look after Iuu, administer the daily cocktail of pills, and just spend quality time with her.

Months later, we slowly began to talk about the months of Iuu's escape.

"You told me on the phone that you didn't love me anymore," I said trying to put on an amusing tone. "Did you really mean that?"

"I tried," she replied, "but it didn't work."

"Just how do you mean?" I inquired.

"You know in the emergency room, after they sedated me, I felt so peaceful. A bright light appeared in the distance and I began following it. Then I heard your voice and from the tone I could sense that you were sobbing and that disturbed the immense peace I felt," she said speaking slowly, pronouncing each word succinctly.

"What were my words?" I asked.

"I vaguely remember that you said 'Iuu' and 'Michael' and 'love' many times. You kept on calling me and calling me so that I started to listen to your voice and stopped following the light."

"If you saw and started following the light, Iuu," I explained tenderly, "that means you were dying."

"I know," she responded looking straight into my eyes, "and it was beautiful. I wasn't afraid of it at all."

I could only but kiss and hold her for how she had said it.

"I need you, Iuu, to be in my life. I cannot live without you. You know that, you had to come back."

We kept looking into each other's eyes, holding hand for a long time and the love just flowed back and forth between us.

The house on Pattaya's Soi Nern Pabwan was eventually sold for 3.2 million bath. With the money Iuu bought us a new home in Bang Lamung in the hills not far from Asian University with a few acres of land, mango and coconut trees.

Months later I dared to broach the subject of the farang Swede, and how Iuu managed to rip him off.

"It was easy. After I had gone with him to his hotel the first night, he simply clutched on to me and I became a sort of mother for him. Anything I suggested he accepted and agreed to. So when I told him I didn't like the hotel accommodation any more because I couldn't cook, we went and I selected a house, then bought a motorcycle, new clothes, and gold and all that. On May 5th, 2004, I found that house in a new village under construction. I liked the upstairs immediately. It was the last one for sale and I decided to make the twenty thousand baht down payment the following day and then we bought it. It's in the name of mother because I couldn't sign being married to you without your signature on the contract."

"Did he ever object to your free spending ways?" I asked.

"No, not at all. He went to the bank every other day and just handed me the bundle of thousand bath notes, trusting me with everything because he didn't speak Thai at all," Iuu explained.

"Wasn't he suspicious at all, or anything?" I was wondering in disbelief.

"You know he had a drug problem and was glad that I turned a blind eye to it. He got his supplies from girls at the beer bars, and I didn't care so long as he kept the money rolling, except one day his mother called."

"Then what happened," I asked.

"His mother spoke to me over the phone and announced that she was arriving in a week to check out our situation, that we were actually going be married, and that the house was in order," said Iuu nonchalant.

"You mean the farang didn't know you were married to me?" I asked with surprise. "What did you tell him when I first surfaced and you moved out of the rented apartment in a hurry. I heard it was all a surprise to him."

"Oh, I said that I owed you money and that we had to run or else there would be big trouble," she replied. "I didn't say you were my husband."

"And, and...?" I egged her on.

"The farang asked how much money I owed, and I said five hundred thousand bath for two years plus three percent interest per month for a total of about a million bath. He decided to call home and have the money wired. I picked it up at the bank two days later, saying I would pay you off in person so that there would be peace from now on," she reported cool and matter-of-factly.

"And where did you put it?" I asked.

"It's in my savings account earning interest. Anything else you need to know?" she declared victoriously.

"And your marriage to him, how did that go," I asked somewhat defensively.

"Easy. I invited a couple of friends and we had a house marriage. Two prahs came from the wat and blessed us for a fee of five hundred bath each. Then I got the marriage certificate, had it framed and hung it up in the bedroom," she declared.

"This is getting fantastic, Iuu. How in the world can you get a marriage certificate when you and I are not divorced," I was getting a little excited.

"I used ours, dummy!" she exclaimed. "This guy Swede, nor his mother, could read any Thai let alone figure out the Buddhist calendar."

"So you were fucking this bastard right under our marriage certificate, and then tell me over the phone you don't love me anymore and want divorce. Gaga..." I was getting carried away a little.

"First of all, Michael, he didn't fuck much. He was into drugs and by the time we went to bed normally stoned and passed out in a hurry. I never loved him, you know me. I went with him because he offered himself and I needed the money."

"What was his mother like?" I continued to inquire.

"She was actually Danish, she said, a small and fat lady, about sixty years old. She ate like a horse. Porridge for her and her darling son in the morning, a big cheese and sausage platter for lunch, washed down with that snaps called Aquavit. She drank nearly a bottle every day. Bought it at Foodland superstore. And for dinner she had a hefty meal delivered by a Scandinavian restaurant. It was all fatty stuff and she washed it down with more snaps, and then lit a cigar in the living room and watched TV with us. The house began to smell bad like a train station restaurant in Germany, remember? I said nothing, because she came for only one week and then left."

"You remember when I found you a second time, this time in your new house…" she didn't let me finish the sentence.

"And that was not nice of you. But what happened. You told Kai's boyfriend that you are my husband, and the friend told the farang Swede and I felt the heat on me. He was not stupid, the Swede, only dependant on me and looked up to me as his substitute mother."

"How did you get out of the bind," I asked.

"I stonewalled, you know me. I simply said 'I don't have to tell you everything' and then asked if he wanted to finish me. As expected he shut up immediately. But he stopped much of the money. From whatever he withdrew at the ATM, he started counting out the thousands. He said ten thousand per week should be sufficient. You really blew a hole in my master plan to start a beer bar business with his money."

"Did he back out or something?" I inquired.

"We didn't get that far. I was under such stress that I landed in the hospital, don't you remember."

"I don't know about stress, Iuu," I suggested, "I think you put a lot of people under a lot of stress yourself by simply absconding and hiding. The aneurysm condition has been with you for a long time and you were lucky, it could have ruptured any time."

"If you do something like that ever again, I will take off to where you can never find me," she began to threaten being her old self again.

"Iuu, that will no longer be possible, and I ask your forgiveness. Can I explain?" I offered apologetically.

"Do what you want. Up to you, Michael," she sloughed me off.

"Iuu, you know that you have two solid titanium clips in your brain to keep your arteries from rupturing again at that particular spot. What you don't know is that there's a GPS chip embedded with one of the clips as well," I politely suggested.

"What's a GPS chip," she wondered.

"Global Positioning System. It's a minute electronic device that can be monitored via satellite telling your location anywhere on earth within three feet of accuracy."

"And I have that?" she asked staring at me with eyes wide open. "How did you get that in there?"

"It was part of the deal with the neurosurgeon. I already had one installed in your old Nokia, but that went over the balcony. Then I ordered a new one from the States and was going to put it in your replacement Nokia, but you said you didn't want anything from me anymore."

"How can you find out where I am?"

"Within minutes from my home computer," I replied.

"This is an added safety feature for you now. If you develop another head problem and don't know who you are anymore or where you are going, then I can have you located within minutes and bring you to safety."

I was putting it on heavy, I realized, when she started bursting out in laughter, came over, hugged and kissed me.

She was a smart woman, I knew. If she couldn't beat you, she would join you and make the best of it. I wasn't quite sure anymore whether I should feel triumphant or ashamed of myself.

A few months later Iuu missed her period and when after another month it still hadn't arrived she took a pregnancy test and then ultrasound. We were going to have twin babies. We were going to be a family at last. Iuu chose the name Jennifer for the girl, and I the name Kalice for the boy.

"What good looking *lukueng* [Eurasians] they will be," said Iuu. "Mother beautiful, father handsome."

"And I will have three Iuus to love. One big Iuu, and two little ones."

Then we hugged.